Unlocking Learning Intentions and Success Criteria

Unlocking Learning Intentions and Success Criteria

Shifting From Product to Process Across the Disciplines

Shirley Clarke M.Ed. Hon.Doc

Associate of the Institute of Education, UCL

Foreword by John Hattie

FOR INFORMATION:

Corwin

A SAGE Company

2455 Teller Road

Thousand Oaks, California 91320

(800) 233-9936

www.corwin.com

SAGE Publications Ltd.

1 Oliver's Yard

55 City Road

London EC1Y 1SP

United Kingdom

SAGE Publications India Pvt. Ltd.

B 1/I 1 Mohan Cooperative Industrial Area

Mathura Road, New Delhi 110 044

India

SAGE Publications Asia-Pacific Pte. Ltd.

18 Cross Street #10-10/11/12

China Square Central

Singapore 048423

Acquisitions Editor: Eliza Erickson

Production Editor: Astha Jaiswal

Copy Editor: Megan Markanich

Typesetter: C&M Digitals (P) Ltd.

Proofreader: Lawrence W. Baker

Indexer: Integra

Cover Designer: Candice Harman

Marketing Manager: Stephanie Trkay

Printed in the United States of America

Library of Congress Cataloging-in-Publication Data

ISBN: 9781544399683

This book is printed on acid-free paper.

SUSTAINABLE FORESTRY INITIATIVE

Certified Chain of Custody

Promoting Sustainable Forestry

www.sfiprogram.org

SFI-01268

21 22 23 24 25 10 9 8 7 6 5 4 3 2 1

Contents

Chapter 10: Science 111

Chapter 11: History and Geography 117

Chapter 12: Examples From Other Subjects 119

PART V: IMPLEMENTATION 123

Chapter 13: Whole-School Development 125

Foreword

By John Hattie

We know the power of high expectations by teachers, we know the power of backward design, we know that sense of achievement when we beat our personal bests, we know that progress through to achievement and not achievement alone matters, we know the high impact of teacher collective efficacy; what unites all these ideas is the clarity, appropriateness, and transparency of the intention and success of any series of lessons. This is provided we tell the students what the intent and success look like and thus make them party to the teaching and learning equations. This is what this book is about.

There have been many meta-analyses asking about learning intentions: having clear goal intentions (7 metas with effect = .51), appropriately challenging goals (6 metas with effect = .59), advance organizers (12 metas with effect = .42); and the impact of success criteria (2 metas with effect = .88), mastery learning (14 metas with effect = .61, and worked examples (2 metas with effect = .37). Collectively, these are among the more powerful positive influences. They are part of the Visible Learning message—teachers working together (with peers and students) evaluating their impact on learning, making clear their expectations of successful learning and investment, particularly by being transparent about their expectations via learning intentions *and* success criteria (LISC), ensuring the LISC are not too hard, not too easy, and not too boring, inviting students to see errors and their lack of success at the outset and during the lessons as opportunities to attain the success criteria, while at all times seeking evidence about the impact we are having on the students' journey to success. Differentiation in this model is having similar LISC for all students (see what Shirley says about this in Chapter 4) but allowing different timings and different progression routes to get there. LISC are anchors to this success—provided we understand how students hear, understand, and are able to do action learning to close the gap from where they start to success and then stopping and smelling the roses of success. This is why a book dedicated to LISC is so critical.

Developing LISC requires skill and knowledge, and we have learned so much over the past decades about how to write, execute, and evaluate them and how to then implement LISC so they become among the most powerful accelerators of learning. They also can be the essence of motivation and engagement—as students can then monitor their progress and see that they are having success in learning such that they want to continue their learning journey and not see classwork as something you finish by handing in to the teacher. This is akin to playing many video games—where the game sets a level (success criteria) based on prior achievement (last score or level) and then provides inordinate opportunities for deliberate practice. When you get to the next level, the motivation to continue to play the game of learning is rewarded, and as we know, many students (and me) can devote large amounts of time and cognitive power to enjoying this learning. My learning has a mission, is not haphazard and random, is not a function of just doing a task, and I know and can enjoy the successes of my investment.

I first met Shirley, the Queen of Learning Intentions and Success Criteria, at a workshop in Chester the day after 9/11. Ruth Sutton had convened many who were working in the area of formative evaluation and assessment systems, and one of the participants entered with a box of her books. Oh dear, another thing to add to the baggage, but this book and interaction changed how I think about assessment. I so much liked Shirley's book *Unlocking Formative Assessment* that I asked her to write a New Zealand edition. As all education is local, kiwis wanted to see their kids, their curriculum, their context. "No," she said, "you write it." So Helen Timperley and I translated the book to kiwi-ese, and it remained a best seller for many years. We have discussed, learned, critiqued each other (now that is fun with Shirley), wined, dined, written a book together, and listened to each other in action, and I have been the beneficiary of listening and working with Shirley—in a similar manner reading this book will allow you to see how she thinks, how she critiques, how she continually wants to improve. And you will be the beneficiary—as will your students.

Shirley has never stopped learning, and one foot is firmly in the realities of classrooms and the other foot is anchored in the research literature. She has learned about product to process success criteria as an important step forward (i.e., "What do I need to do to achieve the learning intention?"), the distinction between rules and tools related success criteria, ensuring skills are linked to precious knowledge, when and how to decontextualize LISC, sharing the development of LISC with students so they not only own them but understand them, the distinction between mastery and performance intentions, and the optimal time for sharing LISC with students.

Take, for example, this big idea—assessment needs to be seen as a feedback mechanism to teachers and students about how much progress they were making toward success. This means being explicit about what it means by success and tying this to the intention of the lessons. Yes, we had known about learning intentions via many names (e.g., behavioral objectives), but these had not been coupled with exemplars of success or with rubrics of steps to this success; we need both learning intentions and success criteria. We know from the behavioral change research the power of intention to implement and by inviting students to see that their investment and learning can lead to even greater intentions to implement. As an ex–music teacher, I could see how using success criteria motivates—by playing the tune, by listening to syncopation, by watching an expert play; it motivated students to want to get to these standards. Surely, we want all students to achieve mastery, so the questions are these: What do you think is mastery? When is good good enough? Have you translated your expectations so that students know only what success in the series of lessons means but can share and enjoy the struggles of the journey toward success?

Oh, say some, I do not know what success looks like until I get there. What chance, then, of your students getting to success, as they drift, comply (or not), think learning is merely do and do, and discover that school learning is completing (to any standard), handing in, and then going out to play? Then this book is for you, as there are skills, knowledge, and deep understanding about LISC that can turn around the compliant, disengaged, disruptive students to having them join those who participate, strive, and thrive in school learning.

Of all the big ideas that underly the rankings in Visible Learning, LISC are among the most important, but they are not easy concepts. This important book unravels the optimal ways to make them work in powerful ways in your class.

Preface

The Background and Lead-Up to This Book

My work on formative assessment, of which learning intentions and success criteria are a major part, has been developing since 1995, when, as a lecturer at the Institute of Education, University of London, I worked with teachers on evaluating and improving students' learning during the learning process as part of the assessment courses I was running.

The mandatory UK National Curriculum had been introduced in 1989, so much of the first few years was taken up with schools trying to find ways of organizing the content into workable schemes of work, or units of study, to make sure everything was covered. At that time, assessment meant summative—testing or observing, or keeping "Records of Achievement" to create "evidence" of learning. How far we have come since then!

I was delving into more "formative" strategies with teachers at the same time when, in 1998, Paul Black and Dylan Wiliam conducted a review of the literature about formative assessment to be handed to national policy makers. They were commissioned by a rebellious group of academics called "The Assessment Reform Group" who were fed up with the UK emphasis on "test, test, test," as if that alone would improve students' learning. Their sixty-page article (Black & Wiliam, 1998a) was summarized into a famous little book called *Inside the Black Box* (Black & Wiliam, 1998b), which still has worldwide sales. Policy makers sat up and listened, and from that moment formative assessment became an expected ingredient in schools throughout the land. So mine and Wiliam's work converged, and we have both been advocating the power and impact of formative assessment ever since.

The term *formative assessment* was confusing for many, often seen as another version of a test, but the definition, from the Black and Wiliam review, was that it is rather a way of teaching and learning, a conceptual framework consisting of the sharing of learning intentions and success criteria, effective questioning, effective feedback, and a culture of high self-efficacy in which students are not compared to others.

That was the starting point, and my mission, ever since, has been to bridge the gap between theory and practice and work with teachers to find effective strategies that could be trialed and shared. I had collected enough stories, examples, and evidence by 1998 to write my first book about this: *Targeting Assessment in the Primary Classroom.* It was just the beginning.

From 2001 I started my "learning teams," the result of requests from local education authorities or school districts, which I still run to this day. Each learning team consists of thirty teachers drawn, in pairs, from fifteen schools, across the age range or grades who meet with me for three days across a year. The purpose of these teams is not just to train those teachers but for them to be able to develop the strategies back in their schools at the end of the year's project. The teachers have to be senior enough to be able to do that and keen enough to experiment with new ideas. School leaders have to be willing to let go of some of their existing policy rules in order to let the teachers experiment with tried and tested powerful strategies.

Back to 2001: I was running six to eight learning teams a year, setting them off in January with strategies drawn from my work with teachers on my courses at the institute (in further years drawn from the findings of the learning teams so far), then meeting them again in June to hear their feedback, organized so that the detail and their anecdotes could be written up by me on my website for more sharing. I gave more input in the afternoon in June; then they came back again in November for more joint feedback and a showcase to local schools of what they had learned and its impact. The gains were two-way: They became formative assessment experts, and I was able to see patterns arising in their feedback, take good examples, identify teachers for video footage (I now have over 130 clips on my website), and see where ideas became significant because they were replicated successfully across all the teams in a year and subsequent years. In 2001 I published *Unlocking Formative Assessment,* the result of those first teams. John Hattie contacted me about the book, and together we produced a New Zealand version.

From then on I ran four to six teams a year, and they still continue. Each year there are new teams, as their impact has become well known. From 2012 I ran teams in Kentucky, Wisconsin, Michigan, and California, when I lived in the United States for two years.

As the years went by, the strategies for the different elements evolved and developed, taking account of new research, becoming more sophisticated. We started dropping things that had seemed helpful at the time, when teachers were first getting to grips with these things, such as acronyms for learning intentions and success criteria.

When I look back at the eight formative assessment books I've written since 1998, I always want teachers to read the most recent book so that they don't go through the initial "finding out" stages and can start with the best we know right now.

Some of the key developments have been as follows:

- Making sure the learning intentions you start with get broken down to lesson level

- Not starting lessons with learning intentions being shared but instead finding out students' current understanding so that the plan for the lesson can be modified if necessary

- Moving from comments in books to more "on the move" feedback to engineer more effective input during rather than after lessons

- Taking account of the impact of cognitive science research when planning for easing the cognitive load in working memory and helping students' long-term memory

- Having mid-lesson learning stops to gauge current understanding and thus to effect in-lesson improvements

- Moving from countless rewards and ability grouping to mixed ability and the learning itself being the reward

- Moving from *product* success criteria to *process* success criteria.

All of these are detailed in my most recent book, *Visible Learning Feedback*, written with John Hattie (Hattie & Clarke, 2019), and in *Outstanding Formative Assessment* (2014), which is still worth a read!

The subject of this book, however, is the last bullet point: the move from product success criteria to process.

How This Book Is Organized

Part 1 of this book is dedicated to setting the scene. In Chapter 1 we will explore the move from product to process success criteria and see a summary of the seven major discoveries we have made about effective learning intentions and success criteria. Chapter 2 will delve into the subject of how students learn, citing the evidence for the use of learning intentions and success criteria.

Part 2 will focus on learning intentions—what they are, how to word them, how to organize and plan for them, and how to share them with students. It can be tempting to gloss over this aspect, but spending time working out exactly what you want students to learn—and where that fits in your plans or syllabuses—has a direct impact on the quality of the lesson or lesson journey you plan.

The next step, in Part 3, is to see how success criteria fit in. These vary according to whether the learning intention is knowledge or skill, whether it is open or closed, and which subject is in focus. These are the findings of many years of teachers experimenting—discovering, at times, how one strategy doesn't work with every lesson. By analyzing these differences, we gain clarity rather than confusion. Although co-constructing success criteria might sound time consuming, I have given many examples of strategies that efficiently do this and shown the great impact co-construction has on students' understanding and ownership of the criteria. The subject of "what makes a good one" is a key element of our teaching, so this is outlined in a number of places, with a walk-through example of whole-class analysis of two contrasting pieces of writing in the English section in Chapter 8.

Differences between subjects follow in Chapters 9 to 12, with more detail for English writing, mathematics, and science than the other subjects. This reflects the main areas teachers in my teams have chosen to experiment with, rather than a deliberate choice made by me. The core subjects always seem to dominate, whether rightly or wrongly, so more is known about those subjects than the others. I believe, however, that the elements of the core subjects can be applied to every other subject.

Implementation is the subject of Part 5, with a range of strategies for whole-school development and staff meetings, illustrated by wonderful teachers' stories about the impact of formative assessment in their schools, especially with the use of learning intentions and co-constructed process success criteria.

I urge you not to miss anything! As you read, the complex jigsaw of how these powerful strategies fit together will become clearer and hopefully inspire you to have a go at enhancing and enriching your students' learning.

Acknowledgments

I would like to thank:

All the teachers in my learning teams since 2001, in the UK and the United States, for their invaluable work in contributing to the evolving practice of formative assessment in action, including learning intentions and success criteria. Without you, my books would not exist!

John Hattie, for squeezing me into his ridiculously busy schedule to write the excellent foreword to this book. Thanks also for the "holy grail" of Visible Learning, now available at visiblelearningmetax.com, and for his support of my work, calling me the "Queen of Learning Intentions and Success Criteria"!

Seamus Gibbons, headteacher of Langford Primary School, London, who, as always, provided me with superb examples and welcome comments to the manuscript

Peter DeWitt, for insightful comments on the manuscript

Kim Zeidler, from Eastern Kentucky University, for links to high school math teachers Jennifer McDaniel and Ashlie Griggs

Stephanie Harmon, from Rockcastle High School, Kentucky, for sending me science examples

Dorothy Grange, wherever you are now, for being the inspiration for success criteria back in 2001: you were the first person I heard talking about the concept and its power

The Corwin team, especially Julie Smith, Ariel Curry, and Eliza Erickson, who first of all empowered me, then helped me through the issues

My husband, John Holmes, for your continued love and support in every aspect of my life and for my daughter, Katy, for just being the light of my life

About the Author

Shirley Clarke (M.ED., HON.DOC) is a world expert in formative assessment, specializing in the practical application of its principles. Many thousands of teachers have worked with Shirley or read her books and, through them, the practice of formative assessment is continually evolving, developing and helping to transform students' achievements.

Shirley's latest publications are *Unlocking Learning Intentions and Success Criteria, A Little Guide for Teachers: Formative Assessment, Visible Learning Feedback* with John Hattie, and *Thinking Classrooms* with Katherine Muncaster. Her website www.shirleyclarke-education.org contains a video streaming platform of clips of formative assessment in action as well as detailed feedback from her action research teams.

PART

I

Setting the Scene

Summary of the Key Messages

1

This chapter is a brief digest of the contents of this book. The details, with many examples, follow in the subsequent chapters, so the purpose here is to cover everything first to give a big-picture understanding. Hopefully this will whet your appetite to find out more about any new concepts, strategies, or ideas.

Why the Move From Product to Process?

First of all, I use the term *learning intentions* rather than *learning objectives* because it is more honest. We can only hope that students will learn what we want them to learn—it is our intention, but it might not be the final outcome. The term *learning intention* is intended to be the focus of a single lesson or series of lessons (e.g., We are learning to understand photosynthesis/We are learning to record observations in a science experiment). In many parts of the United States, these are known as learning targets or standards.

In 2001 I was asked to run a major evaluation project with an Education Action Zone in Gillingham, Kent. The yearlong project had an intervention design: I met all two hundred teachers and introduced the theory and the matching successful formative assessment strategies so far. They went away and trialed everything in their classrooms. Teams of research assistants interviewed teachers, students, and school leaders; observed lessons; and completed questionnaires.

The biggest finding of the entire project was that one-third of the teachers had instinctively created success criteria that showed students the elements they needed to include instead of what the end product should look like. In other words, the success criteria showed the process of student learning rather than the product their learning should produce. These teachers said the impact of *process success criteria* had significantly improved students' achievement but also gave teachers and students something to assess against. It may help some teachers to think of this as "unpacking the standards" so that students know what to do to achieve them. In Example 1.1 there are two examples of product versus process success criteria:

EXAMPLE 1.1: Product vs. Process Success Criteria

We are learning to use effective adjectives:

PRODUCT SUCCESS CRITERIA	PROCESS SUCCESS CRITERIA
I can use at least four adjectives to make my writing more descriptive and interesting.	**Remember:** • Adjectives come before a noun (e.g., the *enormous* egg). • Use your senses to think of words. • Use your thesaurus to find more words. • Use our word wall. • Try to tell the reader something they would not have known (e.g., rushing water, not wet water).

We are learning to find the area of rectangles:

PRODUCT SUCCESS CRITERIA	PROCESS SUCCESS CRITERIA
I can show that I have correctly found the area of rectangles.	**Remember:** • Multiply the length by the width. • You might have to measure the rectangles first. • Your answer must be in sq. cm. (e.g., 15 cm. × 5 cm. = 75 sq. cm.).

From that moment, process success criteria became the obvious way to go, and the UK National Primary Strategy guidelines in 2002 asked for teachers to focus on process success criteria as a result of my Gillingham reports.

What We Know About Learning Intentions and Success Criteria

In the two decades since shifting to process success criteria, our understanding of best practices has deepened. Next you will find a brief description of seven major conclusions we have reached about learning intentions and success criteria. Each of these conclusions will be more deeply explored and exemplified throughout the book.

Learning Intentions Are Derived From Broad Statements, or Multifaceted Statements, Which Are Meant to Be End-of-Year or Key Stage Outcomes

If the learning intentions are assessment criteria, as in the case of the US Common Core State Standards, they don't specify the amount of learning that would need to take place to achieve that outcome. A number of more specific learning intentions need to exist for each of those broad statements, so the first task is to break the standards down to fit timed units of study or schemes of work in order to make the teaching and learning more manageable.

Learning Intentions Can Be Composed of Skills on Their Own, Knowledge on Its Own, or Both— Knowledge Applied via a Decontextualized Skill That Can Then Be Transferred to Any Context

EXAMPLE 1.2: The Three Different Types of Learning Intentions

- *Skill:* We are learning to use adjectives.
- *Knowledge:* We are learning about the history of Thanksgiving Day.
- *Knowledge applied via a skill:* We are learning to write a diary entry (the decontextualized skill) about a child in the Blitz in World War II (the knowledge applied).

Success Criteria for Skills on Their Own

Success criteria for skills on their own can either include *compulsory closed skills* (as in a mathematics skill or a grammar skill) or *optional open toolkits* (as in a fictional piece of writing). Compulsory closed skills would have success criteria built around compulsory steps, and the criteria would begin with the words "Remember to . . ." so students know they must include each step listed. On the other hand, success criteria providing optional open toolkits would begin with the words "Choose from . . . ," indicating to students that they can choose from the options listed, but they do not have to include all of them in their final product to be successful.

Look at these examples of a closed and open skill and the effect it has on whether success criteria are compulsory or optional.

EXAMPLE 1.3: Writing Success Criteria for Compulsory Closed Skills vs. Open Toolkit Skills

Closed skill	Toolkit skill
• Compulsory criteria are included.	• A menu of possibilities for students is provided.
• Once the criteria are mastered, the learning intention is achieved.	• Success criteria don't guarantee quality, but they give suggestions of what could be included.
Learning intention: To use apostrophes correctly (twelve-year-olds—and higher!)	**Learning intention:** To write a story opening (nine-year-olds)
Remember to use apostrophes . . .	**Choose all or some of the following features . . .**
• For possession singular (e.g., My brother's dog—one brother)	• Setting (e.g., dialogue or description, introducing characters, introducing problem)
• When the plural has no *s* on the end (e.g., children's dog/men's dog/people's church)	• Hook the reader. Show, not tell, and suggest what might happen or have happened.
• For possession plural (e.g., my brothers' dog—many brothers)	• Use senses.
• For contractions (e.g., *don't* for *do not*, *isn't* for *is not*)	• Create powerful images for the reader.
• **Remember!** Don't put an apostrophe in *its* when used for possession (e.g., She watched the sea and heard its crashing waves.)	• Use our "what makes good writing" success list.

Success Criteria for Knowledge on Its Own

If the knowledge is imparted with no student product created, there are no success criteria. If the knowledge is researched by the students, the particular research skill will need its own process success criteria.

Applied Skills Must Be Decontextualized

If the learning intention is a skill (to be able to . . .) that has to be linked to a piece of knowledge, it is best for the skill to be decontextualized.

We saw in the early days that if you mixed up the skill with the context, such as "We are learning to write a balanced argument about school uniform," the context (in this case, the school uniform) became the main focus of children's thinking. Asked what they were learning, children would say, "About uniforms." What was more, the next time they had to write a balanced argument about some other context, the skill wasn't able to be transferred, and teachers complained that they had to start again. This was because the process success criteria had listed all the elements about uniforms that should be included instead of what you need in a balanced argument.

So we realized that you have to separate the skill from the context and develop generic success criteria for that skill that would work for any context. When we approach the success criteria this way, it becomes a powerful transferable skill.

Look at the following example:

EXAMPLE 1.4: Contextualized Skills vs. Decontextualized Skills

CONTEXTUALIZED SKILL (WILL WORK FOR THIS LESSON ONLY!)	DECONTEXTUALIZED SKILL (TRANSFERABLE!)
Learning intention: We are learning to write a balanced argument about wearing school uniforms.	**Learning intention:** We are learning to write a balanced argument.
Success criteria	**Success criteria**
Remember to include:	**Remember to include:**
• Why uniforms might be popular	• For and against arguments
• The part that wealth or privilege plays in this issue	• Evidence and examples for your claims
• The place of personal choice	• High percentages, if possible, for the evidence
• How uniforms affect students' opinions of each other	• Quotes if they support your argument
	• Your opinion in the closing
	• Some conclusions in the closing

There Must Be an Equal Status Between Skills and Knowledge

Although the skill and its success criteria must be decontextualized, the knowledge content, or the context, that will be applied via the skill should have equal status to the transferable skill. If you don't treat the skill and knowledge equally, you can end up with a wonderful balanced argument, for instance, with knowledge about the context clearly lacking, so the final piece is not very good! So, in the uniform example, those four bullet points would still be written up for students to see so that they take account of both skill and knowledge.

Consider the following learning intention:

> *Transferable skill:* We are learning to create a tourist leaflet (decontextualized).
>
> *Context/knowledge:* Ancient Greece

We really need to make sure both are treated equally, so the whiteboard might look like this for this lesson:

EXAMPLE 1.5: Treating Skills and Knowledge Equally

Transferable skill: We are learning to create a tourist leaflet.

Success criteria

Remember to include:

- Clear lettering for titles
- Eye-catching front cover
- Pictures to illustrate
- Accommodation
- Places and buildings of interest
- Leisure pursuits
- Costs
- Recommendation quotes

Context: Ancient Greece

- Look at your knowledge organizer and our class resources.
- Use the internet for information.

Younger children might need some pointers:

For example: Don't forget:

- Olympic Games
- Democracy
- Ancient buildings

Learning Intentions at the Secondary Level Can Become Knowledge Heavy

Secondary teachers might be able to assume that the skill with which the learning intention is being applied has been well practiced in earlier years, so their success criteria can focus instead on the knowledge. I might have a learning intention of this, for instance: *We are learning to write an account of/describe the role of the heart in the circulatory system.* For younger students, *learning to write an account* would need to be a skill that required decontextualized teaching: How do you write an account? What does it consist of? But at upper secondary or high school age we might just assume they know how to write an account and, instead, focus on the key points of the knowledge, which become the success criteria:

Remember to include the following:

- The four main functions of the heart
- What the circulatory system does
- The two parts of the circulatory system in detail: pulmonary and systemic

If students do not have basic application skills by the time they reach secondary school, and even if they do, the skills can be revisited by analyzing examples of excellence together as a class.

Students Need to Co-Construct Success Criteria to Take Ownership of Them and Understand Them

This book gives a number of efficient and powerful ways for co-constructing the success criteria. The strategies either consist of demonstration or analysis of examples of previous classes' good examples, and sometimes involve comparing an excellent example with a poor example. Some schools think it is easier to just give students the success criteria—maybe even sticking them in advance in their books. *This is the least effective way of using success criteria.* When teachers simply give students success criteria, they can be hard to interpret and are often ignored. When the students have come up with them by a particularly rich co-construction strategy, they tend to remember them and internalize them. When they have, at the same time, as a whole class together, analyzed an example of an excellent version, students tackle tasks with clear understanding of the steps or ingredients and know what quality looks like. Although the co-construction might take longer with younger children, the time invested in this process is invaluable—their work is instantly improved and of higher quality after they have been involved in the construction and discussion about success criteria.

Analyzing Anonymous Examples of Excellence Is Key to Developing Students' Understanding of Not Just What to Do But How to Do It Well

The role of discussing good examples and modeling what a good one looks like (WAGOLL) cannot be underestimated. By this I don't mean showing them the exact content of this lesson as done by last year's class—although that is usually inspirational with fiction writing—but the same skill with a different context so that they see the main features and get a feel for what excellent writing, drawing, labeling, and analyzing looks like.

Someone recently asked me, "But what if the success criteria don't work? What if I still don't do it properly?" She was referring to a recipe for sourdough bread; she'd followed the recipe (the success criteria), but the bread was still not turning out as it should. This is what might happen when children are simply given success criteria. If we think of this example as a food technology or art learning intention, we would use the co-construction strategy of *demonstrating* at the front, after each stage or step, stopping to ask, "What did I just do?" We would be writing these up as we went along, and the finished list would be the success criteria modeled, analyzed, and discussed. Now the class has all the nuances that might not have been included in the recipe. Imagine analyzing together two short extracts of good writing and discussing what makes one better than the other and why—the turn of phrase or flow of writing can't be summarized in success criteria but can be understood when analyzing excellent examples (for a detailed example of a discussion over two contrasting pieces, see page 95).

My intention in having summarized the key messages in this section is to help the reader see the big picture first: what led to this current understanding and how all the pieces fit together.

There are different ways of writing and stating success criteria across the world, but followers of the development in the UK, and my and Dylan Wiliam's work, will recognize the emphasis on process success criteria. We are continually rethinking and improving our understanding of success criteria—formative assessment in action!

In the end, what matters is that we are doing whatever we can to help students achieve beyond their potential. I have seen, over many years now, that process success criteria linked with co-constructing and analyzing examples of excellence take students to higher levels of achievement and self-regulation—often with immediate impact for that lesson—than we ever thought possible. For too long, children have known what they are learning and what the finished product looks like but not how to get there in an explicit way. This book explains how.

SUMMARY OF KEY POINTS

It might be helpful to mark the following numbers that

- *You feel confirm your practice*
- *Need more explanation (it's all to come!)*

1. Start with a broad learning intention, and break it down into manageable bites for individual lessons or groups of lessons.

2. Success criteria are more helpful to teachers and students if they break down the learning intention into ingredients, steps, or possible inclusions.

3. All learning intentions are knowledge, but some are procedural knowledge (skills) that are the main focus for process success criteria. Skills are ether closed, needing compulsory criteria to succeed, or open, needing a menu of possibilities.

4. Knowledge learning intentions are usually applied via a skill, and students benefit from some key focus points about the knowledge while they carry out the skill. So put focus points for knowledge alongside process success criteria for the skill.

5. Transferable skills should be separated from the context, or knowledge, so that the success criteria are generic, meaning they can be used for any context.

6. Skills and knowledge need equal status.

7. Learning intentions become knowledge heavy after age eleven, but skills still need success criteria.

8. Co-constructed success criteria via effective strategies have more impact than success criteria simply given to students.

9. A key feature of the success of any piece of work students produce is to have whole-class analysis of excellent previous years' pieces of similar student work, finding out what makes them excellent. Comparing a good example with a poor example clarifies what excellence does and does not look like. This, alongside the process success criteria, maximizes student success.

Learning, Not Doing
The Evidence

2

Clarity

Students are often asked by parents, "What did you do today?" A better question is "What did you learn today?" For decades students had been given tasks or activities with no clear understanding of what they were learning other than broad themes (e.g., We did painting/We did some writing/We did the Civil War), so the concept of learning, although assumed, did not appear to be made explicit. So why does it matter? Not knowing affects how you approach the task and whether you can meet the expectations of both the task and the teacher. Imagine you are asked to paint a seascape/compose a short melody/write a letter with no learning intention given. You will have many questions about this task in order to obtain the most favorable assessment from the teacher:

> *Does the weather in the picture matter? Can I have other things in the picture like boats, people, or hills? What are you looking for?*
>
> *Can I use any instruments? What do you mean by short? Does it matter if it is atonal? Can it be any style? What is its purpose? How will it be assessed?*
>
> *Can the letter be to anyone? What should the letter be about? Does it matter if it is friendly and chatty, or should it be polite and serious? How will I know if I've got it right?*

These questions usually manifest themselves in the classroom by students either (a) asking you what they have to do, even though the activity has been explained or (b) taking a lead from the person nearest them who is the best bet for getting things right and copying their approach.

Now imagine the difference if students are given the following learning intentions:

- We are learning to create watercolor washes. Context: a sky, sea, and land seascape

- We are learning to compose an eight-bar piano melody in baroque style. Context: any keyboard instrument

- We are learning to write a formal letter. Context: a letter of complaint after food poisoning in a restaurant

The clarity of the learning intention answers the students' questions. Not only does it clarify purpose for the students but it makes planning the lesson more focused for the teacher. Here is a possible walk through my lesson planning for the first learning intention: We are learning to create color washes.

I could do the following:

1. Demonstrate creating watercolor washes, co-construct the success criteria for this skill with students as I demonstrate, and write up the different steps.

2. Have the students practice the skill before moving on.

3. Have the class look at pictures of seascapes.

4. Present an excellent example of washes and a poor example—both from last year's class—and have students compare the two, analyzing what makes the difference between them.

5. Ask students to paint their own by using the success criteria they co-constructed and the knowledge they have gained.

6. Be on the move as students work, looking for instruction points, maybe adding to the success criteria, and encouraging students to share any insights.

One example of the impact of the lack of a learning intention is a clear memory I have of my middle school science homework one day. We were asked to repeatedly place our hands in hot then cold water at home and write up what happened. I did this faithfully and noticed that my hands were changing color: to red then white then mottled. I duly noted the different changes of color and received a curt comment at the foot of my writing when it was returned to me: "But what did you notice about your ability to feel the change in temperature?" I remember thinking, "Why didn't you tell us it was about temperature?" Of course, I assumed it was my fault for not being able to understand what the teacher wanted: students will always assume that any problems in their learning are their own fault.

Teachers often worry that science learning intentions will "give the game away"(telling the students the answer to something we want them to discover on their own during the lesson), but this doesn't have to be the case. Rather than state "We are learning that . . ." the wording can be "We are finding out what happens when. . . ." Making this small shift ensures the purpose is clear, but the investigation is still intact. The learning intention for my homework that day should have stated, "We are finding out how reliable the human nervous system is in detecting variation in temperature."

Knowing How to Get There

In the UK, back in 1990, when the England and Wales National Curriculum (which noted what to teach, but now how) was first introduced, teachers all started with *product* success criteria. My Gillingham study of 1991, involving 560 elementary school students and their teachers, revealed that teachers who instinctively gave students *process* success criteria saw greater learning gains. Of course, students need to know the expected final outcome, but process success criteria show students how to get there.

EXAMPLE 2.1: Product vs. Process Success Criteria From the Gillingham Project

LEARNING INTENTION	PRODUCT SUCCESS CRITERIA (OUTCOME EXPECTATION)	PROCESS SUCCESS CRITERIA (ENABLES THE LEARNING)
To be able to use papier-mâché	You will have made a solid bowl of papier-mâché.	**Remember to:** • Tear up newspaper into small strips. • Create the required shape out of chicken wire, or use a balloon. • Mix wallpaper paste. And so on . . .

(Continued)

(Continued)

LEARNING INTENTION	PRODUCT SUCCESS CRITERIA (OUTCOME EXPECTATION)	PROCESS SUCCESS CRITERIA (ENABLES THE LEARNING)
To write an effective characterization	Someone who reads it will feel they really know the person.	**Choose to include:** • Their hobbies and interests • Their likes and dislikes • Extrovert or introvert? • Examples of their personality (key point) • Their appearance if it shows something about their character • Their attitude to others • A back story to illustrate their character
To identify odd and even numbers	Your answers will be mostly correct, showing you understand the difference between odd and even numbers.	**Remember to:** • Look at the last digit in the number to check the pattern. • Divide the number by two to check (even divides equally, odd has one left over).

Process success criteria are a breakdown of the learning intention, giving either the compulsory process steps needed or the possible ingredients for students to choose from. Without success criteria, how are students to know which elements they should include or emphasize? How will they know how their work will be judged? How will the teacher know all the elements that need to be taught or for students to have feedback about?

Once the learner has process success criteria, they have a framework for a formative dialogue, with peers or adults, which enable them to do the following:

- Know what the learning intention means.

- Know the *compulsory steps* involved with a closed learning intention (e.g., to find percentages of whole numbers) or the elements of a particular writing form (e.g., a newspaper report).

- Know the *possible ingredients* for an open learning objective (e.g., a ghost story opening).

- Identify where success has been achieved and where help might be needed.

- Be clearer about where improvements can be made.

- Have a basis for peer discussions.

- Discuss strategies for improvement and self-regulation.

- Reflect on progress.

The Evidence for Learning Intentions and Success Criteria

Visible Learning Findings

In Hattie's groundbreaking synthesis of meta-analyses (www.visible learningmetax.com), sharing *learning intentions* has an effect size of 0.51 and is categorized as having the "potential to accelerate student achievement." Sharing *success criteria* has an effect size of 0.88 and is categorized as having the "potential to considerably accelerate student achievement."

Formative Assessment

Learning intentions and success criteria are key elements of formative assessment (see Figure 2.1): a conceptual framework of instruction and learning strategies, which, when combined, give students maximum opportunity to achieve beyond their potential.

FIGURE 2.1   The Key Elements of Formative Assessment

Formative Assessment: The Key Elements

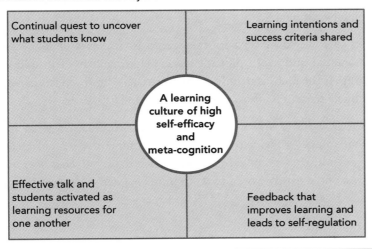

Formative assessment in action includes the following:

- The learning intention is the starting point for the teacher's or teacher and students' *planning,* although the starting point of a *lesson* is often to plan a five-minute prior-knowledge question for the class to discuss in their pairs (see examples on page 46) while the teacher eavesdrops, then deciding whether the plan for the lesson needs any on-the-spot rethinking.

- The learning intention is broken down into mini goals or ingredients, commonly known as *success criteria,* most effective when co-constructed with students.

- Using published or old anonymous examples of excellent and "not so good" student work for class analysis allows the concept of *quality* to be known for the focus learning intention.

- Talk partners; good questioning; and on-the-spot self, peer, and teacher feedback, often via "mid-lesson learning stops" enable *improvements to be made* during the learning.

Mastery and Performance Goals

All schools use mastery goals and performance goals. Performance goals are focused on how the learner is *performing (getting an A grade),* whereas mastery goals focus on what the learner is *learning (how to solve simple equations).* By students knowing learning intentions and having constructive feedback that relates to that learning intention (Ames & Ames, 1984; Butler, 1988; Crooks, 1988; Deevers, 2006; Hillocks, 1986), they are more likely to achieve both the mastery and performance goals, as mastery and effective feedback can be seen as the route to high performance.

If schools overfocus on performance goals, students often become demoralized and avoid difficult tasks, believing that their ability is lacking. If the focus is mainly on mastery goals, however, students are less likely to switch off from learning (Rolland, 2012).

Carol Dweck's (1989) work on motivation summarizes what happens if you get students to focus only on competitive structures such as grades (*performance orientation*) rather than on *what they have learned* and what they need to do to improve (*learning orientation*; see Figure 2.2):

FIGURE 2.2 Performance Orientation vs. Learning Orientation	
PERFORMANCE ORIENTATION *(I want the best grade/merit mark/to be first.)*	**LEARNING ORIENTATION** *(I want to work hard/I want to learn and know how to improve.)*
Belief that ability leads to success	Belief that effort, practice, and input leads to success
Concern to be judged as able and to perform	Belief in one's ability to improve and learn
Satisfaction from doing better than others or succeeding with little effort	Preference for challenging tasks
Emphasis on interpersonal competition and public evaluation	Derives satisfaction from personal success at difficult tasks
Helplessness: evaluates self negatively when task is difficult	Applies problem solving and self-instructions when engaged in tasks

The Process of Learning

Hattie and Timperley (2007) describe the process of learning and feedback as three elements:

> Where am I going? (Knowing the learning intention)
>
> How am I going? (How am I doing so far? Helped by the success criteria)
>
> Where to next? (How could I improve?)

Black and Wiliam (2009) have three similar elements:

> Where the learner is going (knowing the learning intention)
>
> Where the learner is right now (How am I doing so far?)
>
> How to get there (success criteria and knowing what excellence looks like)

Both models draw on the "closing the gap" theory made famous by Sadler (1989) drawing on the work of Ramaprasad (1983). The learner has to do the following:

- "Possess a concept of the standard (or goal or reference level) being aimed for.

- Compare the actual (or current) level of performance with the standard.
- Engage in appropriate action which leads to some closure of the gap" (Sadler, 1998).

Student Ownership of the Learning Intention

Sadler doesn't say "know the goal" but instead says "possess a concept of the standard (or goal . . .)." This is achieved by not only knowing the learning intention but also understanding how it breaks down into criteria that help the learner achieve the goal. Co-constructing success criteria by analysis of excellent examples or comparing good and poor examples makes the concept of the goal even clearer. Once students know the goal, the success criteria, and what excellence does and does not look like, they are in full possession of the goal. Without all of these, it would be like being given instructions to make a chocolate cake with no recipe, instructions, or picture of how it should look, or it would be like trying to build a table with no clear goal (size, material, style?), criteria for success, or a chance to look at good and poor examples and what makes the difference.

In order to judge the quality of a student's achievement, the teacher must have a clear understanding of what the learning intention means, what quality for that learning intention would look like and be able to compare a student's performance to that concept. It is not enough for the teacher to hold this idea of what success looks like, however, as the feedback would only be one way, limiting the student's ability to develop independently. *The student* must also understand the learning intention and the definition of quality held by the teacher so that he or she can monitor their progress during its production—the ability to self-regulate, a characteristic of deep learning.

Success criteria are a breakdown of the learning intention, most helpful when they focus on the process and give the rules or tools that enable the student to achieve the learning intention. Wiliam and Leahy (2015) state the following:

> Process success criteria can be particularly helpful to students if they break the process that students are expected to follow into a number of smaller, more easily managed steps.

We need to remember, of course, that not all success criteria are steps, as they are sometimes ingredients, not necessarily in chronological order, and can be optional suggestions rather than compulsory elements. More of this later!

The success criteria give a basis for student self-regulation and feedback and demystify the steps or ingredients needed to achieve success. They differ for skills and knowledge and often between subjects—hence, the many examples throughout this book.

Simply *giving* students success criteria is not as powerful as *co-construction*. Effective strategies for co-construction nearly always involve analyzing good examples or comparing good and poor and identifying what makes one better. This makes the process rich in not only helping students to internalize the success criteria but also to see what excellence does and does not look like.

Transfer to Long-Term Memory

In order to have any chance of transferring new learning to long-term memory, we know, through cognitive science research, that "memory is the residue of thought" (Willingham, 2009). It follows, therefore, that students need to be focusing their learning and thinking on the learning intention and success criteria—what we want them to learn and how to get there. Without this clarity, they could easily be preoccupied with other aspects of the task or what they believe to be important rather than what we want them to actually think about.

SUMMARY OF KEY POINTS

1. The emphasis should be on learning, not doing, with clear learning intentions.
2. Process success criteria state the steps or ingredients during the process of learning, which will provide a structure for self- and teacher assessment. Product success criteria state the expected outcome.
3. Learning intentions and success criteria have high effect sizes in meta analyses.

4. Learning intentions and success criteria are one part of the conceptual framework of formative assessment.

5. By focusing on learning intentions and success criteria, students are more focused on mastery goals than performance goals, which will ultimately improve their final grades.

6. Sadler's (1989) "closing the gap" conditions include knowing the goal but also possessing a concept of the goal, achieved by process success criteria and knowing what good ones look like.

7. The cognitive science research on memory indicates that "memory is the residue of thought," so we need students to be thinking about learning intentions and success criteria as the main focus of their learning.

Learning Intentions

A Closer Look

Planning the Learning   3

The Big Picture

Organizing Students' Learning and Application of Skills and Knowledge

When we think about a learning intention, we focus on these essential questions:

- What do I want students to learn?

- How do I articulate that?

- What would be a good way of learning it?

- What do I think some excellent finished products would look like?

The learning intention, and/or lesson starter question, helps students focus on how much they already know about this topic, anchors them throughout the learning process, and encourages their self-regulation—being able to not only self-assess but also to see where and how improvements can be made.

Everything we want students to learn, whether for one subject or for topic-based learning, consists of two major elements:

- Specific skills, concepts, and knowledge, which need to be taught and practiced (often the surface stage of learning)

- Applications of those taught specifics, which need analysis of excellent examples to develop a greater understanding of what a good final product looks like (usually the deep stage of learning)

Both of these elements are needed, of course. We teach skills, concepts, and knowledge; students practice; then, usually, they apply what they have learned. I think of this simple division as "taught specifics" (or the "bits" we teach) and "linked applications." The following table shows some random taught items and how they might be linked to an application. It is when students can apply their learning, especially in different contexts, that we start to believe that they have deep understanding and have really learned it.

EXAMPLE 3.1: Taught Specifics and Linked Applications

TAUGHT SPECIFIC LEARNING INTENTIONS (CLOSED SKILLS OR KNOWLEDGE)		LINKED APPLICATION LEARNING INTENTIONS (OPEN SKILLS OR KNOWLEDGE)
To use adjectives and adverbs	⟹	To write a complete story
To punctuate speech	⟹	To use dialogue in writing
To use Pythagoras's theorem to find an angle	⟹	To use Pythagoras to solve problems
To know the key events of the American Revolutionary War, or American War of Independence	⟹	To create an opinion piece on the advantages and disadvantages of the war
To learn the position and order of sharps and flats in music	⟹	To write music in different key signatures
To know Spanish vocabulary related to food and restaurants	⟹	To use food and restaurant vocabulary in Spanish prose

Open and Closed Learning Intentions

Another way of looking at these specific skills and the applications of those skills is "closed" (for the taught specifics) and "open" (for the applications). I find this distinction useful when it comes to determining what mastery and excellence looks like. Closed learning intentions, like you see in the first column of Example 3.1, have straightforward steps or rules to follow to achieve mastery. Teachers often use "Remember to" as the lead-in to success criteria for closed learning intentions, because students need to follow them all to achieve the learning intention. Open learning intentions, like the ones listed in the second column, are more difficult to give compulsory rules for, because there are usually many ways in which they can be achieved. The success criteria for these open learning intentions often begin with "Choose from," because they offer a menu or toolkit of possibilities students can choose from. Mastery of open learning intentions is harder to define, especially when any prose writing is involved. This is why open learning intentions not only need process success criteria but also class discussions about what excellence looks like by analyzing last year's good examples and deciding what makes them good.

In planning the learning, there needs to be a balance between the taught specifics (closed learning intentions) and applications (open learning intentions). The convention is to teach the specifics first, then ask students to apply them. Some teachers prefer to ask students to do the application first, especially in mathematics, in order to find out what they already know and what needs to be taught. The principle of finding out what students already know is fundamental, not just for whole units of work but for every lesson—this often looks like a short question or statement discussed by the class in pairs for five minutes while the teacher eavesdrops and gleans their current understanding. The outcome could be that yesterday's learning has been remembered or not remembered, or, for a new lesson, the planned lesson might need modification as most students know more than was expected, or the reverse!

Thinking of learning intentions as taught specifics and applications allows us to clarify some issues:

Firstly, *it is impossible to make all learning intentions specific* and explicit: *application* learning intentions are necessarily broad as they exemplify students' grasp of their knowledge.

Applications are commonly used for students to practice their skills in action and for summative assessment (How well has this been understood?) by teachers and students alike.

Secondly, *it is of little use making ongoing summative judgments (How many students have understood this?) of the taught specifics,* because they look as if they can do it at the time. The acid test of the taught specifics is in the applications: These are the only valid and reliable contexts for summative decisions. Ongoing assessment for taught specifics is best focused around formative assessment: establishing where success is taking place and reinforcing that as well as identifying improvement needs as skills are being developed.

Coverage

When planning content coverage, the convention that seems to work best is to start from what you want students to learn (from the syllabus or curriculum) and give broad headings to categorize that learning (e.g., the seasons/algebra/*Romeo and Juliet*). Many schools plot an entire unit's learning intentions in advance, breaking the learning intentions down from the broad standards or statements, showing what will be covered each week, and making sure they focus in on the key skills and knowledge they want the students to encounter.

There are many different ways of formatting planning, and what works for one teacher or school might not work for another. I show two contrasting teachers' plans here. Steps for planning individual lessons in the various subject areas will be covered in Part 4. What matters is being clear about what you want students to learn rather than being constrained to a specific planning format or template.

Planning Examples

The following example, from Langford Primary School, is for seven weeks' history lessons for seven-year-olds about the Great Fire of London. Teachers in Langford have agreed on this format together and find the elements very helpful. They adjust and modify these plans at the end of the topic to help inform the next teacher who uses it.

EXAMPLE 3.2: Teacher's Plan for a Seven-Week History Topic With Seven-Year-Olds

LESSON SEQUENCE	QUESTIONS STUDENTS CAN CONFIDENTLY ANSWER BY THE END OF THIS LESSON	LEARNING INTENTION FOR THIS LESSON
1	Links to what the children already know: Team 1 arranged trips to central London. What places have you seen in London when you visited central London? Link with fire brigade visits: Why can a fire be dangerous?	**Learning intention:** To ask questions Share the new topic and learning journey. What do we know? What do we think we know? What do we want to know?
2	What was the plague? How many people did it kill? How would that have affected London? Why did it spread so quickly? Why couldn't it be stopped?	**Learning intention:** To understand why the plague spread so quickly
3	Name different sources that we can use to find out information about past events. Why are some sources more reliable than others?	**Learning intention:** To know different sources of historical information

LESSON SEQUENCE	QUESTIONS STUDENTS CAN CONFIDENTLY ANSWER BY THE END OF THIS LESSON	LEARNING INTENTION FOR THIS LESSON
4	Where did the fire start? Why did it start? When did it start? How quickly did it spread? How long did the fire burn? How did they stop the fire?	**Learning intention:** To know key facts about the Great Fire of London Children retrieve and collect information from a range of sources to answer questions. www.fireoflondon.org.uk/game/
5	When did the fire start and end? When did St. Paul's Cathedral burn down? When did King Charles II become king? When did he die? When was the plague?	**Learning intention:** To order key events about the Great Fire of London T1—Henry Croft/Victorians before or after the Great Fire of London?
6	What changes were made after the Great Fire of London? How had and did the weather impact the speed at which the fire spread?	**Learning intention:** To understand why the fire spread so quickly **Materials:** Wooden houses, thatched roofs
7	What impact did the Great Fire of London have on the city of London? How did they rebuild the city? What new laws were introduced? How do we protect ourselves and our houses from fires now?	**Learning intention:** To know changes that were made in London after the Great Fire

By contrast, here is a teacher's plan for a high school science focus. This is what works for Stephanie Harmon at Rockcastle High in Kentucky:

EXAMPLE 3.3: Teacher's Plan for Thermal Energy Science Topic With Fifteen- and Sixteen-Year-Olds

The science standard the teacher addresses in this plan, noted in the first row of her planning document, is referred to within the Next Generation Science Standards (NGSS) as a performance expectation. Within it, all three dimensions of the NGSS are addressed—Science and Engineering Practices, Disciplinary Core Ideas, and Crosscutting Concepts. One of these dimensions—the Science and Engineering Practices

(Continued)

(Continued)

(SEP)—includes the type of process skills that the teacher will want to address. The process skill targeted here is "plan and conduct an investigation."

	PLANNING AND CARRYING OUT INVESTIGATIONS	HS ENERGY
Standard addressed: NGSS HS-PS3-4	Plan and conduct an investigation to provide evidence that the transfer of thermal energy when two components of different temperature are combined within a closed system results in a more uniform energy distribution among the components in the system (second law of thermodynamics). *[Clarification Statement: Emphasis is on analyzing data from student investigations and using mathematical thinking to describe the energy changes both quantitatively and conceptually. Examples of investigations could include mixing liquids at different initial temperatures or adding objects at different temperatures to water.]* *[Assessment Boundary: Assessment is limited to investigations based on materials and tools provided to students.]*	
Science and Engineering Practices	Planning and carrying out investigations to answer questions or test solutions to problems in 9–12 builds on K–8 experiences and progresses to include investigations that provide evidence for and test conceptual, mathematical, physical, and empirical models. • Plan and conduct an investigation individually and collaboratively to produce data to serve as the basis for evidence, and in the design decide on types, how much, and accuracy of data needed to produce reliable measurements and consider limitations on the precision of the data (e.g., number of trials, cost, risk, time), and refine the design accordingly.	
What (Learning intention)	We are learning to design an investigation of how heat flows between different materials and the air around us. **Context:** Heat transference between gloves and our hands	
How (Success criteria)	Remember to: • Decide which materials should be tested, how many trials to run on each material, and how long (time) each trial should run. *(Use conversation cards to discuss these choices with your talk partner.)* • Decide which tools are most appropriate for collecting this data—which will make the most reliable measurements? • Identify limitations on the precision of the data *(by using the accuracy and precision cards).* • Use the data as evidence to determine which material or material combination keeps my hand the warmest. • Organize data in a logical manner. • Use data to support your work.	
Possible scaffolds	• Use the specific tools that are given instead of a wide choice. • Use the anchor chart or visual for comparing and contrasting accuracy and precision.	

Planning Flexibility

Although a planning framework is important and useful, flexibility is a necessary aspect so that coverage doesn't become more important than the needs of the learning. Planning too many learning intentions or too much content can result in never doing anything thoroughly enough to move from surface to deep to transfer. Nuthall (2007) discovered that students need three exposures to new learning to have any chance of remembering it, so sometimes sacrificing coverage for learning takes precedence—always compromising at the teacher's discretion and professional judgment. Gardner (1993) stated that "the greatest enemy to understanding is coverage." The number of learning intentions to be covered seems daunting, but many are learned incidentally alongside others, and many need much shorter time in the classroom than is actually devoted to them, especially in elementary schools where all-encompassing topics or projects can take up more time than would be necessary.

Knowledge and Skills

It's All Knowledge

We know that all learning intentions are, in fact, knowledge. Think of any skill (e.g., tying shoelaces), and you can see that it consists of knowledge steps. The curriculum is all knowledge—even those things we call skills are, in effect, *procedural knowledge*. That said, I continue to differentiate between skills and knowledge for ease of reference. Knowledge is factual (to know that . . .), and skills are procedural (to know how to . . .), with learning intentions that look like this:

Knowledge

To know properties of 2D shapes (knowledge)

To know the key events of the Vietnam War (knowledge)

Skills

To be able to write a letter (skill)

To be able to solve quadratic equations (skill)

TASK!

Decide now whether these are *skills* (procedural) or *knowledge* (factual):

- Times tables facts

- Writing a characterization

(Continued)

(Continued)

- The impact of steam power
- Solving quadratic equations
- Using watercolors
- Properties of 2D shapes
- Multiplying with the column method
- Key events of the Cold War

(Answers are at the end of the chapter!)

We usually apply knowledge with skills like this:

> *To know* key facts about the attack on Pearl Harbor in 1941 (knowledge)—applied with
>
> *To write* a newspaper report, letter home (skill)—Context: one week after the attack

Learning the Knowledge

Knowledge is either taught or researched, with extracts from textbooks or "knowledge organizers" commonly given to students to aid recall and to provide a reference to key facts during the learning. Key reference points can be given as knowledge success criteria when the learning intention is mainly knowledge based, which is often more prominent in secondary classes. Figure 3.1 is a good example of a knowledge organizer; it was created for eleven-year-olds studying earth, space, and forces for an earth science focus.

It is helpful for students to see and receive instruction about the big picture: exemplifying the knowledge and how it is applied in skills:

As you know, we have been learning about the human body. So far we've studied the skeleton and the major organs. Today we will be learning about our five senses and why we need them. Later on we will be looking at the digestive system and reproduction. We will be doing some experiments about our senses and learning how to record observations. By the end of this lesson, you should know a lot about the senses and we will have together created the success criteria for recording scientific observations.

FIGURE 3.1   A Knowledge Organizer

Langford Primary
The best in everyone™
Part of United Learning

Earth and Space and Forces

Earth and space key vocabulary

Atmosphere	The air all around Earth
Black hole	An object with gravity strong enough to suck anything into it—even light
Constellation	A group of stars that make a shape (they look like connect the dots)—usually named after mythological characters, people, animals and things
Eclipse	This is when one celestial body cuts off the light of another—like when the moon covers the sun for a brief moment.
Galaxy	A large group of stars. Our galaxy (called the Milky Way) includes the sun.
Geocentric	The belief that the Earth is fixed at the centre of the universe
Heliocentric	The idea that the Earth and other planets revolve around the sun, which is the centre of the solar system
Orbit	The path that an object moves around a second object or point. For example, Earth orbits the Sun.
Planet	An object bigger than an asteroid orbiting a star. Our solar system has eight planets
Solar system	The sun, the eight planets and any other celestial bodies that orbit the sun
Universe	All the matter and energy out there—this includes the Earth, galaxies, solar systems, you, and everything else.

The solar system

Key People

Nicolaus Copernicus	An early astronomer, scientist and priest in Poland, thought the sun was at the centre of the solar system
Isaac Newton	Born in 1643, Isaac Newton is considered one of the most important scientists in history. Newton developed the theory of gravity.

Earth and the moon are both spherical in shape. The rotation of Earth causes day and night.

Forces

Gravity	Gravity attracts all objects towards each other. How much gravity an object has depends on how big it is—to be specific, how much mass it has.
Water resistance	Water resistance is friction between your skin and the water particles. It is able to act against the effects of gravity.
Air resistance	Air resistance is a type of frictional force that occurs between gas as and the surface of solids.
Lever	A lever is a simple machine that can give a mechanical advantage.
Pulley	Pulleys are made by looping a rope over one or more wheels. They are often used to lift heavy objects: pulling down on one end of the rope creates an upward pull at the other end.
Gear	Wheels with teeth that slot together. When one gear is turned the other one turns as well. If the gears are different sizes, they can be used to increase the power of a turning force.

Source: Langford Primary School, Hammersmith and Fulham, London.

In the following examples, knowledge is broken down, then applied with a skill. Notice that the skills are all transferable to any relevant knowledge, not just this context.

LONG-TERM KNOWLEDGE INTENTION (APPLICATION)	SHORT-TERM KNOWLEDGE INTENTION(S)	TRANSFERABLE SKILL
To know the play *Romeo and Juliet* ⇦	To know the first two scenes of *Romeo and Juliet* ⇦ To understand the character of the nurse To identify language features that convey emotion	To write a characterization (Context: of any key character in the first two scenes)
To know all about our local area ⇦	To know where our town is on a map ⇦	To be able to use a map to find a destination
To know how the human body works ⇦	To know about the senses and their purpose ⇦	To be able to record observations
To know significant events of America's role in World War II ⇦	To know the impact of the bombing of Hiroshima ⇦	To select and organize historical information

Breaking Down the Skills

Skills are most helpful when broken down into the steps or ingredients that we call success criteria. They help students know what they have to do during their learning to achieve the learning intention.

Long-term intentions are usually broken down to lesson-by-lesson, specific learning intentions, illustrated by the following:

EXAMPLE 3.4: How Learning Intentions Break Down Into More Specific Intentions

LONG TERM (OFTEN SEVERAL YEARS!)	SHORT TERM (INDIVIDUAL LESSONS)
To be able to punctuate correctly ⇨	To use question marks To use commas Etc.
To be able to design a science experiment ⇨	To record observations To plan the variables To write up a method or experiment Etc.

Decontextualizing Transferable Skills

Many skills can be transferred to different contexts, as shown in Figure 3.2:

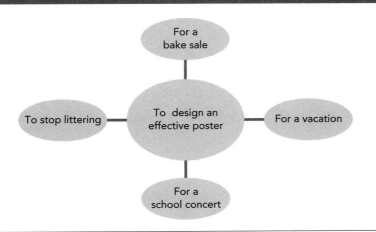

FIGURE 3.2   How a Learning Intention Can Be Applied to Different Contexts

For a bake sale

To stop littering — To design an effective poster — For a vacation

For a school concert

Instead of telling students they are learning to design a poster for, for instance, a holiday to Paris, instead first discuss what *makes an effective poster*, co-constructing the success criteria. Once these are generated, they can be used every time that skill comes up, regardless of the context. Transferable skills are powerful, and by keeping them and revisiting them for different contexts, students start to internalize the criteria so that, eventually, they know automatically what you need to include in a science experiment or poetry analysis.

Obviously, when the *effective poster* criteria are used, students also need knowledge success criteria for the linking context; otherwise you could end up with all the success criteria for a poster fulfilled but with inadequate knowledge content. There could be two columns on the whiteboard/flip chart—one for the skill success criteria and one for today's knowledge content:

EXAMPLE 3.5: A Transferable Skill Alongside Key Focus Points for the Linked Knowledge

Learning intention: To design an effective poster (transferable skill)	**Learning intention:** To know facts about Paris as a tourist destination
Remember to include:	**Think about:**
• All key information	• Sightseeing highlights (e.g., Eiffel Tower)
• An easy-to-read font	• Examples of accommodation
• Good contrasts	• Excursions
• Eye-catching design	• Travel possibilities (e.g., the Metro)
• Main message in the biggest lettering	• Food and drink
• Pictures if useful, which emphasize the message	• Culture (museums, history, theater, opera, etc.)

One teacher of eleven-year-olds experimented by doing the same lesson twice—once with the skill contextualized and again but with the knowledge separated from the skill. Here's what she said:

> *Context included*: They were asked to write Goldilocks from a different perspective. The students got side-tracked with the features of the tale, like details about the characters, and did not include a different perspective adequately.

Decontextualized: For another lesson, she asked the students to first generate, with her, success criteria for "writing a traditional tale from a different perspective." It was as if a light had switched on. There was a dramatic impact on the quality of their writing after they had co-constructed the elements (process success criteria) for this generic learning intention. The teacher later tried the same thing in history and found the same thing happened. She said the whole experiment had been "amazing."

This impact has been repeated to me by many teachers in my mixed phase action research teams.

Bringing Skills and Knowledge Together

When knowledge and skills are combined, students have access to the success criteria for the skill and key points for the applied knowledge. They don't have to wonder what the teacher is looking for, and they have been involved in the co-construction of the success criteria (see Chapter 6 for detail about co-constructing), maximizing their understanding and engagement. Imagine something like Example 3.6 on the whiteboard for the learning intention of writing a newspaper report on the attack on Pearl Harbor.

EXAMPLE 3.6: Transferable Skill Alongside Linked Key Knowledge

Learning intention: To write a newspaper report (transferable skill)	**Learning intention:** To know about the attack on Pearl Harbor (key points for this context only)
Remember:	Use your knowledge organizer or textbook.
• Punchy headline to hook the reader	or
• Subheading	Use Google.
• Summary in first paragraph: Where, why, who, what, when?	**Consider:**
• Clear explanation in chronological order	• Number of casualties
• Make accessible complex information	• Ships and planes destroyed
• Use the third person	• USS *Arizona*
• Past tense	• Reason for the attack
• Use quotes if they will add to the report	• How the US government responded
• Last sentence to be thought provoking	• Reaction from citizens

The newspaper report skill can be applied over and over with any context. The knowledge link is clearly for this lesson or lessons only.

Overemphasizing either skills or knowledge, rather than bringing them together, can result in poor quality work from students—either lacking in the elements of the skill in question or lacking in the appropriate knowledge content, so the clear message is to *make knowledge and skills have equal weight when considering what excellence looks like.*

For many years skills have been overemphasized as a reaction to rote learning of knowledge from previous decades. Children knew a lot of facts but not necessarily how to use them.

Cognitive science studies from the past ten years have highlighted a number of facts about children's learning and the role of working memory and long-term memory. Knowledge has been redefined as an all-encompassing title for everything we learn, but teachers find it helpful to think of procedural knowledge (to know how to . . .) and factual knowledge (to know that . . .). Both are equally important in learning. In the UK this has led to more emphasis on what we teach in order to bring knowledge and skills into some alignment. I have seen schools thinking more carefully about what they want students to finish a unit of study knowing and remembering—not just trivial details but key profound messages. In a topic on World War II, for instance, we might have previously focused on the main events, vocabulary and so on, whereas now, alongside those elements we might have planned some *big* questions that we want students to be able to articulate at the end of the topic, such as the following:

- What were the causes of World War II?

- Why were so many lives lost?

- What was put in place after the war to stop wars from happening again?

Instead of a number of separate lessons that can be easily forgotten, these questions become the guiding knowledge and purpose in teaching this topic at all.

To reemphasize, make "to know that" and "to know how to" have equal weight—one without emphasis on the other loses its value and purpose.

The Differences in Planning for Primary and Secondary

When children are elementary school age, much of their learning is focused on the development of reading and writing. There are skill learning intentions and success criteria for almost every lesson. By the time they are established in middle school, however, the focus becomes more geared to the application of the critical knowledge required, and basic writing skills are assumed. Instead of focusing on the criteria for a diary entry, a letter, a retelling, or an opinion piece, for instance, a secondary teacher might, in a science lesson, ask for a write-up of how heat is transferred from the hand to the glove after discussion and instruction. The success criteria will consist of key knowledge they need to consider in their writing. How to actually write a science account becomes assumed knowledge, as it will usually have been taught and developed in earlier years. This is why secondary education becomes more knowledge focused—the means of applying knowledge has been taught and worked on for many years from children's first marks on paper, to constructing sentences, to adding adjectives and other devices and learning the different genres and nonfiction styles of writing.

This isn't to say that those basic skills won't need revisiting in middle or high schools, especially in terms of defining what good examples look like. Knowing what excellence looks like via analysis of comparative pieces from previous students plays a vital role throughout our education. Imagine if you had been able to, at university in a seminar group, analyze together two or three examples of excellent degree level assignments—for instance, deciding what makes them good, maybe comparing one with a poor example and discussing what made the difference. I believe we would all have been significantly impacted and informed about expectations in an explicit form. Such discussion should be seen as a vital investment rather than another thing to fit in.

Getting the Wording Right

Start Big, Then Refine

The starting point for any *planning* of learning should be the broad learning intentions, then their breakdown into more precise lesson-based learning intentions, then deciding what activity will help fulfil this most effectively. It can be tempting to carry on with favorite activities and try to link learning intentions with them. The only way this will work will be if you rethink the instruction of the activity to adhere to the learning intention. Tenuous or superficial links make the purpose of the learning unfocused, and students might be thinking about other aspects of the task rather than what you want them to really think about. This links again with Willingham's (2009) "memory is the residue of thought." Sometimes the source of learning intentions, in a written document, can seem overwhelming. Once you have decided what you want to be the main learning for the lesson, it makes life easier for all concerned if the learning intention shared with the students is as clear as possible. Clarity doesn't necessarily mean close detail: if your learning intention is an application, it will be deliberately broad to see how much students know and can do.

Learning intentions, without first explaining the long-term learning intention, can also lead to students missing the point: "To understand the effect of banana production on the banana producers" was a learning intention I once saw given to a class of ten-year-olds at the beginning of the lesson. The teacher had chosen to focus in on the journey of a banana to illustrate her bigger learning intention, which was to understand the extraction of resources. A banana was a random choice made by the teacher for the context. She didn't actually want them to know all about bananas, just their journey from start to finish and the wider issues.

Given the first learning intention, it is likely that students will believe that extraction of resources is only an issue about bananas. Students asking during the lesson what they were learning told me they were learning about, of course, bananas. By starting with the broad learning intention "to understand extraction of resources," then asking for a brainstorm of all the different products we could find out about, students will see that this is a learning intention that can be applied to many different contexts. They can now focus in on the journey of a banana as the learning intention for this lesson—perhaps bringing in other products along the way to compare issues.

Just reflecting on "What do I really want them to learn for this lesson?" usually presents the words you need to frame the learning intention. Let's imagine you want them to learn how to convey empathy in a persuasive letter—then that is your learning intention. Imagine you want them to learn how to add numbers on a number line—then that is your learning intention. Sometimes the learning intention can escape you: One of the teachers in one of my teams reflected how she had told her students that they were learning to sort shapes and said how frustrated she had been that all they could talk about was the shapes. I asked her why she was disappointed, as that was what she had told them they were learning. She replied that she wanted them to be able to use a Venn diagram. She instantly realized that "to use a Venn diagram" should have been the learning intention. Now we see how the right focus for the learning intention has a big impact on the plan for the lesson as this teacher also realized she didn't have to give all the students just shapes to sort.

What Do I Really Want Them to Learn for This Lesson?

If you follow the starting point of "What do I really want them to learn for this lesson?" you will be able to construct a learning intention that is focused and clear. I have listed several clear learning intentions, defined each one as skill or knowledge, and identified what the related success criteria will look like:

- **To solve quadratic equations**
  - Skill learning intention
  - Requires process, step-by-step, compulsory success criteria
- **To know how landslides, volcanic eruptions, and earthquakes cause changes in rocks**
  - Knowledge learning intention
  - Requires knowledge teaching and closed success criteria
  - When this knowledge is applied, it will be applied via a transferable skill, such as "writing an explanation text."
- **To find the area of 2D shapes**
  - Skill learning intention
  - Requires process, step-by-step, compulsory success criteria
- **To use effective adverbs**
  - Skill learning intention
  - Requires process, optional success criteria (a menu of options)
- **To know the key events of July 4, 1776/the Gunpowder Plot in England**
  - Knowledge learning intention
  - Requires knowledge teaching and closed success criteria
  - When this knowledge is applied, it will be applied via a transferable skill, such as "writing a newspaper article."
- **To use watercolors**
  - Skill learning intention
  - Requires process, optional success criteria (a menu of options)

- **To define the concept of *main idea* in writing**
  - Skill learning intention
  - Requires process, optional success criteria (a menu of options)
  - Will be applied through a transferable skill, such as "writing a creative story"
- **To use evidence to support an analysis of what a text says explicitly**
  - Skill learning intention
  - Requires process success criteria and key knowledge criteria for the linking text
- **To define negative exponents and use them to rewrite exponential expressions**
  - Skill learning intention
  - Requires process, step-by-step, compulsory success criteria

Part 3, on success criteria, gives many examples of learning intentions and success criteria for both knowledge and skills.

SUMMARY OF KEY POINTS

1. Learning intentions consist of "taught specifics" and applications of those.

2. Students need at least three exposures to new learning to remember it.

3. Coverage should be viewed with flexibility to ensure learning takes place.

4. All learning intentions are knowledge: factual (to know that . . .) or procedural (to know how to . . .)—otherwise known as knowledge and skills.

5. Learning intentions need to be broken down to lesson level.

6. When skills are linked with a context or knowledge, they should be decontextualized when co-constructing success criteria so that it becomes a generic transferable skill.

7. Skills and knowledge should have equal status to ensure optimum achievement.

8. Learning intentions become more knowledge heavy at secondary level, with transferable application skills often assumed to have been learned at the elementary or primary level.

9. Ask "What do I want them to learn for this lesson?" to plan the precise learning intention for lessons.

ANSWERS TO CHAPTER 3 TASK!

Times tables facts: Knowledge

Writing a characterization: Skill

The impact of steam power: Knowledge

Solving quadratic equations: Skill

Using watercolors: Skill

Properties of 2D shapes: Knowledge

Multiplying with the column method: Skill

Key events of the Cold War: Knowledge

Sharing Learning Intentions With the Students

4

In-Lesson Organization

Timing

Although it seems appropriate to start a lesson with the learning intention already on the whiteboard, it is more appropriate to start with a prior knowledge quick question to find out how much students know already or have remembered from previous lessons on this topic. Asking students to discuss answers with their partner while you eavesdrop on their conversations often reveals current understanding and can make the difference between continuing with the plan for this lesson, modifying it in some way, or abandoning it altogether! It is the teacher's discretion as to when would be the most appropriate time to reveal the learning intention—when, by not knowing it, it would negatively affect the students' understanding and performance.

Some examples of prior knowledge template starters are shown in Ex.4.1. If you look at the learning intentions in that table, you see they are abbreviated (e.g. the first one, in the classroom, would be written up as 'We are learning to be able to identify squared numbers' but because of limited space in the table I've abbreviated it to 'Squared numbers'). Abbreviations of the learning intentions are supplied here but would not be written up for students until prior knowledge discussion had taken place. For more examples of prior knowledge templates, see *Visible Learning: Feedback,* by Hattie and Clarke (2019).

EXAMPLE 4.1: Examples of Prior Knowledge Starter Questions Before Learning Intentions Are Revealed

QUESTION TEMPLATE	EXAMPLE	EXAMPLE	EXAMPLE
Range of answers	**Learning intention:** Squared numbers What is 5 squared minus 3 squared? **Discuss:** 11, 16, 2, 13, 2 squared	**Learning intention:** Plant growth What makes plants grow? **Discuss:** Water, sand, electric light, chocolate, sunlight, milk, chips	**Learning intention:** Persuasive writing Which strategies are likely to persuade? **Discuss:** Evidence, bias, empathy, bullying, objectivity, bribery
Agree or disagree?	**Learning intention:** The Vikings' battle clothing This picture shows a Viking. Agree or disagree? Say why . . .	**Learning intention:** Retelling and interpreting text Goldilocks was a burglar. Agree or disagree? Say why . . .	**Learning intention:** Finding percentages 45 percent of 365 is greater than 54 percent of 285. Agree or disagree? Say why . . .
Odd one out	**Learning intention:** Properties of 2D shapes Which of these is odd? Triangle, square, circle, rectangle, pentagon. Say why . . .	**Learning intention:** Adverbs and adjectives Which of these is odd? Slowly, carefully, bright, happily. Say why . . .	**Learning intention:** Nutrition and food groups Which of these is odd? Nuts, meat, eggs, lettuce, fish
What went wrong?	**Learning intention:** Punctuation recap The girl stared after some minutes rain fell on her head she wore a rain hat Discuss . . .	**Learning intention:** Electrical circuits (Picture of a circuit not connected properly) Discuss . . .	**Learning intention:** Multiplying by partitioning $18 \times 5 = 10 \times 5 + 9 \times 5$ $= 50 + 45$ $= 95$ Discuss . . .

Video 4.1: Watch Mark with seven-year-olds finding out if they understand place value using Dienes blocks.

Should All Students Have the Same Learning Intention?

If we want to have high expectations for all students, they should all have the same learning intention and success criteria. A mastery curriculum is standard in Far Eastern countries with high achievement rates in world comparisons. Many published schemes now lead with this approach, especially in mathematics. Differentiation with a mastery approach is most successful when the task is supported to enable students to access the learning intention and success criteria. Table facts, for instance, can be given to students who don't yet know them—when the lesson focus is to learn a particular mathematical skill that requires table facts. Marginalizing students from vital skills because they don't have basic facts holds them back and can result in students moving up from elementary or primary school without those skills. Similarly, rather than giving certain students different work to do because they find it difficult to write, give them a partially completed finished product within which they write so that they are still engaging with the focus learning intention and success criteria.

By the time students are in secondary or middle school, they tend to be ability grouped, which is intended to reduce issues of differentiation. Even with a tracked or streamed class, however, there is usually a wide range of achievement, so the same principles apply. Interestingly, it is illegal to group by ability before the age of fifteen in Finland, one of the highest achieving countries in the world. Studies for at least thirty years have shown that the impact of ability grouping on achievement is minimal, but its impact on self-efficacy is profoundly negative (Chiu, Chow, & Joh, 2017; Hattie, 2002; Oakes, 1992). Ability grouping has an effect size of 0.12 in Hattie's (2009) Visible Learning synthesis of meta-analyses.

Writing Down the Learning Intention

Although it might be tempting to ask students to copy the learning intention into their books or notebooks, for young students this can take too much time away from their learning. I always recommend that the learning intention gets written up on the whiteboard at the appropriate time but that students simply write a title in their books, which is an abbreviated form of the learning intention. If students can write fluently and quickly, it doesn't seem to matter either way.

Asking or Telling Students Why We Are Learning This

Asking students why they think we are focusing on a specific learning intention really comes down to the professional judgment of the teacher. The value of this discussion often varies by subject area. For example, when we ask this question in an English classroom, the response will always be similar—to make our writing more interesting or correct, or to make our reading better—so the discussion seems to have little value. In a mathematics classroom, however, asking students, "Why are we learning this?" can have greater purpose, because you can explain the real-life application of some of the seemingly pointless elements. The same is true for science and other subjects that have clear real-life links.

In-Lesson Feedback and Evaluation

On-the-Move Feedback

While students are engaged in their independent or cooperative learning, an effective strategy is to be "on the move," pen in hand, giving students feedback while they are in the moment and there is time for improvement or corrections to be made or spotted. This saves teachers having to write comments on students' books after the lesson, when it is often too late to have any significant impact. Being clear about the learning intention of the lesson can be betrayed by the teacher, however, if his or her comments when walking around the room focus on other features. The point is to be transparent about what you are looking for—the learning intention and success criteria for the task and maybe the everlasting success criteria that are always in play, such as spelling, grammar, and punctuation as long as this doesn't create less focus on the learning intention and success criteria. In mathematics this might be correct formatting, checking calculations, and so on. Of course, where creativity is involved, and especially at secondary age, students might go beyond or even subvert the success criteria, as in the case of fictional writing, using them as suggestions that allow for individual brilliance.

Using the Learning Intentions for Self-Evaluation and Whole-Class Evaluation

It is helpful to (a) ask students, during the lesson, to indicate how they think they are doing by using traffic light cards or fans that they lay out on their desks and (b) stop to check up on the whole class understanding by having a quick multiple-choice question on the whiteboard for which students show their answers by writing on their mini whiteboards or dry erase boards and holding them up. This allows for some improvement or input to take place while the learning is in progress. Asking students to evaluate their learning against the learning intention at the end of the lesson can also be useful, either by young students simply taking turns telling their partner what they were most proud of and what they still need more input or practice for, or the same with older students in oral or written form. This can either be written straight into their books or onto an exit card, such as a mock phone template or a more traditional exit card in which students demonstrate their learning for this lesson.

Another common strategy is to highlight the learning intention or its abbreviated form in students' books *if the student has demonstrated the expected standard for that lesson or cycle of learning.* Notice that I have not suggested that this be highlighted to show it has been *learned.* Achievement in a lesson is demonstration of performance only. Learning can only be seen if it is still remembered sometime later and can be applied successfully, usually in different contexts. Wiliam (2018) said the following:

What looks like good instruction may not be effective in the longer term and the distinction between learning and performance matters: learning requires long term retention of knowledge, whereas performance simply means doing well on a particular task.

The Impact of Sharing and Clarifying Learning Intentions

The following examples are derived from teachers in my learning teams and are exemplary of twenty years' worth of examples we've collected since teachers have begun to share learning intentions in the ways described in this chapter. These examples show the clear impact of clarifying and sharing learning intentions.

Three-, Four-, and Five-Year-Olds

- Retelling: whereas before students would simply retell the story of "The Three Little Pigs," they now use story language, like "once upon a time" and "happily ever after."
- "Making Father's Day cards" was changed to "Learning to cut accurately": the result was more attention to the skill and subsequent transferring of that skill.
- "Making treasure maps" was changed to "Mapmaking": the quality of work was higher, and their talk was about mapmaking rather than treasure.
- "Making snowflakes" was changed to "We are learning to cut with scissors." Classroom assistants behaved differently with students, saying "Think how you are using the scissors" rather than "What a lovely snowflake you've made."
- "Sorting shapes" was changed to "Using a Venn diagram." Students talked about the Venn diagrams rather than the shapes.
- "Making robots" became "Using joining skills," so junk modeling focused around joining rather than talking about robots.

Six- and Seven-Year-Olds

- One teacher focused on "explanation" with the context of a car traveling down a ramp. Students were able to explain very clearly what they had learned. A parallel teacher had taught the same lesson but had made the learning intention "Making a car go down a ramp." Those students could only say things like "I made a car whiz down the ramp!"

- One class did information writing with the context of dinosaurs. A few weeks later, the students remembered the success criteria and were able to transfer the skill to a different context of elephants.

Eight- and Nine-Year-Olds

- One class did explanatory texts in literacy and were able to transfer this skill to a science report on how rocks are formed.

- One teacher changed "Taking the temperature between our toes" to "'Reading a thermometer" with the context of "hot parts of the body."

- A teacher started a unit on persuasive language with the context of making a poster. She asked the class for ideas for the context, which resulted in her scrapping her planning and focusing the whole unit around the context of the TV program *The Apprentice*. They were highly motivated yet focused on the skills involved.

- One teacher used the "Life skill" for the learning intention and "This time only" for the knowledge (e.g., Life skill = drawing perspectives; This time only = houses).

- In a PE lesson, a teacher emphasized the sequencing involved in floor work, which the students were then able to transfer to large apparatus. Usually she has to start again because it all looks so different.

Ten- and Eleven-Year-Olds

- A child with Asperger's syndrome told the teacher that the learning intention had made him happy because he could think about what he was going to learn.

- Students wrote a nonchronological report about St. Lucia. When they later had to write a report about the countries taking part in the World Cup, they were able to immediately use all the skills learned from the previous report.

- Writing a persuasive leaflet, one child recognized that he had done something like this before (a transferable skill) and said, "This is exactly the same but a different subject!"

- Teachers in one team felt that they had moved away from "Doing the Romans" and were now looking at a set of skills within that context.

- One teacher had a key skills geography curriculum and was using the context of rain forests. When this had been covered without key skills in the past, the students would end up knowing a lot about trees and animals but have no understanding of the skills involved. They studied a local area for a week and then showed students images of the rain forest. Students were able to then identify the positive and negative aspects of the rain forest and were now using geographical vocabulary instead of context vocabulary.

- In history, "Designing an Egyptian banquet menu" was changed to "To know what foods the Egyptians ate," with the context of designing a banquet menu. In the past, they had focused on the creation of the menu, but with the new learning intention they understood what they were learning.

- After estimating and measuring with angles, a class then did the same with capacity. Because the focus was estimating and measuring, they were not scared at a new context. Students have gained confidence as a result.

Twelve- to Eighteen-Year-Olds

Physics

o One teacher found that students could now recognize the same skill being practiced again in a different context (e.g., transport, electricity).

Mathematics

o One teacher changed "Finding the area of shapes" to "Applying a formula to find the area of shapes." Each lesson dealt with a different shape, but a formula was being applied each time, which was a more successful approach. This has made students more independent.

o "With ninth grade (fifteen-year-olds), you deal with the same formula in different contexts all the time. Before I separated the learning intention from the context, students did not realize they could use the same formula across different aspects of mathematics. I think you could cut down the number of math instruction intentions considerably by focusing on transferring the same formula."

English

o An intention of "Expressing empathy" meant that students were clear about what they had to do and did not get bogged down with the wrong things.

o In a special school, a class of fourteen-year-olds was reading *Macbeth* for a test. The students focused on the research and presentation skills involved. Weeks later a science teacher, working with a completely different context, said that the students' research and presentation skills were excellent, and they had told her about how they had done this in their English class.

o In one school, 80 percent of students increased their grades by at least one as a result of the use of process success criteria.

o There is a positive impact on behavior the more student independence and confidence increases.

SUMMARY OF KEY POINTS

1. To gauge current understanding, start lessons with a prior knowledge question to eavesdrop paired discussions.

2. Give the class the same learning intention and success criteria, but differentiate their access to the success criteria by modifying or supplementing the task.

3. Don't waste children's time by asking them to copy out whole learning intentions into their books—abbreviated titles suffice.

4. "Why are we learning this?" should be used when there is a real-world link.

5. The learning intention can be used throughout and at the end of a lesson for self-evaluation and teacher on-the-move feedback.

Success Criteria

A Closer Look

Process Success Criteria

A Framework for Learning and Self-Regulation

5

Defining Process Success Criteria

There are two main types of success criteria: process and product. Having a basic understanding of both types will be helpful before we move into learning how to develop effective process success criteria.

Process success criteria are a breakdown of the lesson learning intention with the purpose of helping students to achieve the learning intention. They should help students know what to include and whether those things are compulsory (for closed learning intentions) or optional (for open application learning intentions). If the success criteria are co-constructed with the students, using excellent or poor anonymous old examples (in a different context) as a vehicle to generate them, the success criteria lead to greater learning gains than if the criteria are simply given to students.

Product success criteria tend to be a reiteration of the learning intention or its elements (e.g., you will have measured, recorded, and calculated the average temperature) and are useful to show students the final outcome expectation but not how to get there.

There is no reason why both can't exist, but product success criteria often consist of a single statement, and process success criteria break down that statement into building block elements needed, or to choose from, in order to achieve a successful final product. The product success criterion is a starting point, while process success criteria provide a road map for students to help them know how to achieve the learning intention.

Planning Process Success Criteria for Skills

If we are to teach a particular learning intention, the starting point, as discussed in Part 2, is to be clear about what you want them to learn—whether skill, knowledge, or both—and how you will express those in words. Also, planning the success criteria to be able to achieve that learning intention means you, the teacher, are clearer about what needs to be taught, practiced, and learned. Some elementary teachers can find it difficult to decide the steps or ingredients for a subject that they feel they are not expert enough in, but the big question then is this: How are you going to teach it if you are not sure exactly what students need to do? Secondary teachers often find success criteria easier to define because of their immersion in and knowledge of single subjects. Primary teachers usually have someone with a subject expertise in their school who they can consult or online resources that have success criteria broken down (make sure they are process not product!).

Once you have a good idea of the success criteria, the next stage is to decide how to co-construct with the class (see Chapter 6). This is worth every second spent, as students then understand and have ownership over the success criteria. They will also often be written up, as they are constructed, in the students' own words, making them even more accessible.

What Might Happen as You Start to Plan . . .

1. A good starting point for skill success criteria is to imagine the steps or rules the students will need to take or follow to achieve the task. This works well for closed learning intentions as in skills for mathematics, grammar, and punctuation, where there are compulsory elements to achieve success (e.g., to multiply three digits by two digits using the column method/to use semicolons accurately).

2. It could also be, when considering some open skill learning intentions, that you realize there are no compulsory elements at all—only suggestions of what students might include, as in a piece of creative writing (e.g., to create a descriptive setting for the start of a horror story).

3. Then there are learning intentions that are everlasting—not usually the specific intention of any one lesson—and are usually displayed in the classroom as a permanent reminder (e.g., every time we write/every time we do mathematics/every time we do science).

Writing Learning Intentions and the Implications for Their Success Criteria

Closed learning intentions lead to mastery, and open learning intentions require a toolkit of possibilities and a discussion of what excellence looks like.

My realization about the difference between open and closed skill learning intentions, as mentioned on page 34 (open and closed learning intentions), came about because teachers were telling me that students were ticking off all the success criteria for their writing—thus, believing that they had achieved success. However, teachers found that checking off each criterion was not necessarily an indication of whether the final product was an example of an effective piece of writing. By contrast, when students ticked off all the success criteria for a mathematics learning intention, it was a good indication of success as long as their calculations were accurate. The reality was that—even with the success criteria followed whenever students have to write anything—there was, and always will be, an obvious difference in quality between students' final products that cannot be captured in the success criteria.

We started to see that you actually *could* tick off or check all the success criteria for a mathematical algorithm, punctuation, grammar, and other "closed" skills and know you had achieved success, whereas a piece of writing, any writing, depends on your understanding of what excellence looks like. These are success criteria that students are learning to improve for the rest of their lives! Ask any author if they have achieved mastery of their writing, and they would probably say they are continually learning. This means that although a child might have used the success criteria options, their inclusion doesn't guarantee quality.

There is a difference between nonfiction writing (e.g., an invitation, an explanation text, a balanced argument) and fiction writing (e.g., a characterization, a descriptive opening).

Nonfiction writing has compulsory ingredients for its structure. For example, an invitation must indicate who it's to, who it's from, where the event is, and at what time. These are vital "Remember to" ingredients and important for students to know, but these do not guarantee excellence in the finished product—only that the right elements have been included. So students will benefit from analyzing old examples of good and bad invitations as a class to pinpoint the question of quality.

Fiction writing can only have "Choose from" success criteria, because there aren't any compulsory elements. For example, optional success criteria for a piece of suspense writing could include a scary setting, the main character alone or remote, or including short sentences for impact. The menu of options gives students ideas and techniques that have been identified in previous, anonymous pieces via whole-class discussion.

We realized that having the whole class analyze and discuss excellent examples of finished work and having them compare and discuss good writing samples with poor writing samples was the key to helping students see what excellence might look like. The more examples of good work they see, the better their understanding. This is why avid readers tend to be the best writers in your classroom: they encounter multiple examples of what excellent writing might look like, so they are more able to apply that knowledge in their own writing.

As students analyze successful samples and compare good and bad examples as a class, you can work with them to co-construct some open success criteria that characterize the successful writing samples.

EXAMPLE 5.1: Examples of Open Application Learning Intentions That Require Whole-Class Analysis of Last Year's Excellent Examples

We are learning to:

- Write a persuasive argument/letter, etc.
- Write effective similes/metaphors/personification, etc.
- Solve a numerical/geometric problem.
- Compare data/reports/pieces of artwork/etc.
- Analyze a poem for meaning.
- Distinguish between fact and opinion in historical accounts and give evidence.
- Empathize in writing/role playing.
- Devise an effective sequence using balance and traveling in gymnastics.
- Use effective adjectives/adverbs/complex sentences, etc.
- Write a characterization.
- Draw an effective conclusion in science.

Include Knowledge Key Points Alongside Skill Success Criteria

Knowledge learning intentions are often placed alongside the skill learning intention, as the knowledge is needed for the skill to be successful. So although I might focus a lesson on being able to, for instance, write a historical account from two points of view, students will also need to have instruction about the knowledge they are using for this skill (e.g., German, English, and American perceptions of the purpose of World War II).

Video 5.1: Watch Seamus with eleven-year-olds comparing two good paragraphs to discuss what quality looks like.

Knowledge learning intentions need key focus points, as in the following examples. These are the teacher's notes, but this is the aim for what would end up being displayed at the front while the students are working. The notes are meant to guide the co-construction conversation, and the wording might change as the students and teacher co-construct the items. Chapter 6 details some of the most effective strategies for co-constructing success criteria with the class.

EXAMPLE 5.2: Transferable Skill Success Criteria Alongside Linked Knowledge Key Focus Points

LEARNING INTENTION: We are learning to write a book review (transferable skill)	**LEARNING INTENTION: To know the book *Matilda* (knowledge)**
Remember to include: • Summary of the story (but no spoilers) • Key characters • Best/worst part • Age relevance • Any humor • Message of the book • Why you do or don't recommend it	**You need to know:** • Her character and her powers • Her family life • Her battles to read • Miss Trunchbull's character • Matilda's savior, Miss Honey • Her happy ending • The message of the book

LEARNING INTENTION: We are learning to write a formal letter (transferable skill)	**LEARNING INTENTION: To know about the impact of plastic use in food packaging (knowledge)**
Remember to include: • The sender's address • The address of the recipient • Dear Mr./Mrs./Ms. and name	**You need to know:** 1. Evidence about the effects of plastic in the environment (e.g., recycling issues, use of fossil fuels, wildlife, pollution)

(Continued)

(Continued)

LEARNING INTENTION: We are learning to write a formal letter (transferable skill)	LEARNING INTENTION: To know about the impact of plastic use in food packaging (knowledge)
• Formal sentence starters (e.g., I am writing to inform you . . .) • At the end "Yours faithfully" or "Yours sincerely" if name known • Sender's name • Points made clear	2. Examples of unnecessary packaging in school cafeteria 3. Biodegradable alternatives

LEARNING INTENTION: We are learning to measure and construct an angle (skill)	LEARNING INTENTION: To know the names of angles below 180 degrees (knowledge)
Remember to: • Line up the protractor accurately on the line. • Start from zero, and choose an angle. • Make a sharp pencil mark. • Join the left side end of the base line to the pencil mark. • Label the angle.	**You need to know:** • Angles smaller than 90 degrees are acute. • Angles at 90 degrees are right angles (makes an *L*). • Angles bigger than 90 but less than 180 are obtuse.

Everlasting Learning Intentions

Don't forget to note your everlasting learning intentions, which are usually displayed in the classroom as a permanent reminder, because they are not tied to a single lesson.

EXAMPLE 5.3: Everlasting Success Criteria, Usually Permanently Displayed

EVERY TIME WE WRITE	EVERY TIME WE DO MATHEMATICS
Remember to check: • Spelling • Punctuation • Handwriting • Grammar	**Remember to:** • Make an estimate first. • Line up columns. • Check your calculations in a different way. • Put the correct units in the answer (3 cm., not just 3).

EVERY TIME WE WRITE	EVERY TIME WE DO MATHEMATICS
Decide: What impact do you want your writing to have on the reader? What will do this best? Look at our "Techniques for Good Writing" poster (using senses, use of similes, metaphors, etc.). Look back over your writing as you go, improving any parts there and then. Read your writing quietly aloud to yourself to hear whether it works and if the punctuation is correct.	• Separate each calculation. • Number the different calculations. • Decide if it will help to use jottings or record in any way. • Decide if it will help to use a resource. • Think if there is more than one way to approach the problem . . . which would be most efficient?

SUMMARY OF KEY POINTS

1. Process success criteria answer this question: What do I need to do to achieve the learning intention?

2. When the learning intention involves writing prose, for any subject, the process success criteria will be compulsory for the structure of a nonfiction piece but optional for fiction writing.

3. Skills have process success criteria; knowledge learning intentions have key focus points.

4. Each subject can have everlasting success criteria (i.e., "Every time we do mathematics/write/etc.") on permanent display in the class-room that apply to all lessons for that subject.

Co-Constructing Success Criteria $\large 6$

Why Take the Time to Co-Construct?

When students have a stake in the generation of success criteria, they are much more likely to internalize, use, and remember the criteria. Simply asking students what they think the success criteria would be for a learning intention, however, is a long-winded and tedious experience, probably with poor outcomes. Over some years, I have collected, from teachers, an ever-growing number of excellent strategies for co-constructing success criteria with students. These strategies not only enable the success criteria to be generated efficiently and effectively but also have the advantage of simultaneously helping students see and understand what excellence for this learning intention might look like. The time it takes to co-construct is a precious investment that pays dividends in reaping long-lasting understanding.

Co-constructing success criteria leads to the following:

- Students becoming more independent in self-regulation
- Students having a checklist to follow or choose from
- Students having more ownership over their learning
- Students deciding which criteria they need more input for or practice of

- Higher achievement occurring when students have seen and analyzed good examples
- Older students teaching younger students more effectively
- Higher achievers teaching lower achievers more effectively

Strategies for Whole-Class Co-Construction

When analyzing excellent, or not-so-good, examples of student work with the whole class, start by projecting the examples to the front of the room. Whether you use a document camera or a smart board, the important thing to note is that the entire class is looking at a single example together, and it is displayed in a way that students can read the words, or see the details, so they can effectively analyze what makes an example of student work successful or unsuccessful.

Before we move on to the strategies, it is helpful to note what won't work well. First, don't ask the students to come up with the success criteria without using one of these strategies. It will be like pulling teeth. Second, don't show them just one poor example and ask them to improve it. They need to see excellence next to poor, or several excellent examples, to identify the elements and features of a successful finished product.

Strategy 1: Analyze Excellent Products

1. Show students two or three examples of excellent final products.

2. Ask students, "What features do you see here that make these examples excellent?"

3. Take student responses, and write up their ideas that are specific to the learning intention. These will become the co-constructed success criteria.

This is useful when students will be doing any nonfiction or fiction writing as well as prose writing in any subject. Before they start the task, show them one or two excellent examples from last year's class, and have a whole-class discussion about what makes them good. Keep in mind that, with writing examples, it is better to have short extracts rather than long pieces. Make sure they are anonymous pieces—preferably from last year's class—although many teachers make these up themselves if they can't retrieve any examples of excellence.

EXAMPLE 6.1: Using Strategy 1 to Co-Construct Success Criteria for a Piece of Suspense Writing

To co-construct criteria for suspense writing, for instance, I might write two short texts on the whiteboard:

Mia stood in the dark and listened. She could hear something breathing. . . .

The huge parking lot was empty. Not a soul was in sight. Julia's car was the only one left. As she walked toward it she could see something or somebody standing beside it. . . .

The reason we provide more than one example is to make sure students don't copy the style of the text we analyzed but can see different versions of excellence. This is particularly important in writing.

Read the first sentence aloud; then ask for students to talk to their learning partner for thirty seconds to identify one technique the author has used to create suspense. Take their responses, writing up the ideas as you go. Make sure you take only the elements that are specific to suspense, rather than those features that would be appropriate for any writing.

The success criteria for both examples could be as follows:

- The main character(s) is alone.
- The setting is threatening (dark, fog, derelict house, woods, remote place, etc.).
- The threat is unnamed (somebody, something).
- The verbs chosen (e.g., *breathing*) suggests something scary.
- Use of ellipsis
- Short sentences
- Show not tell.

Students might need you to start them off if they can only see features like "The sentences are short." An effective strategy is to say, for the first criteria, "Does it say, 'Mia *and all her friends* stood in the dark and listened'?" They will quickly see that being alone makes it have more suspense.

Similarly, for the other criteria, we could ask, "Does it say Mia stood in the *brilliant sunshine* and listened?" "Does it say 'She could *hear her baby daughter* breathing'?" "Does it say she could hear something *chirping*?" and "Does the sentence end with *an exclamation mark*?"

By comparing the nonthreatening version with the original sentence, they understand and appreciate the techniques the author has used.

Strategy 2: Compare a Good and Bad Example With the Whole Class

1. Hand out or project two contrasting pieces next to each other for the whole class to see (could be photographs or video if performance or art related).

2. Read out loud if the pieces contain writing.

3. Ask students to quickly decide which is best and vote.

4. Give thirty seconds for pairs to decide one feature that makes one example better than the other.

5. Take their responses, and write them up to form the success criteria, co-constructing where necessary.

6. Give a further thirty seconds for discussion if all the criteria are not mentioned in the first round. Add any more that they might not have noticed.

The juxtaposition of excellent next to poor is powerful in making clear what is and what is not good. Seeing what makes an effective poster, for example, would be clear to students if they are shown a professional poster next to a poor poster, in which there is missing information, unclear fonts, noncontrasting color, all the same size writing, and no eye-catching images. Keep students' work from previous years, and you will have access to anonymous excellent and poor examples that become a great resource for co-constructing success criteria.

Instead of asking young students to draw a self-portrait by looking into a mirror (very difficult to transfer 3D to 2D), present them with a self-portrait done by a talented teaching assistant (TA) or teacher next to a self-portrait that you have drawn, deliberately making it awful—no eyebrows or neck, wrong color hair, etc.—which will make them laugh but again makes clear what should be included by the juxtaposition of the two self-portraits.

This strategy can be used effectively for many learning intentions, as in the following examples:

EXAMPLE 6.2: Using Strategy 2 to Co-Construct Success Criteria for Writing Director's Notes

We are learning to write director's notes (fourteen-year-olds).

Context: *Romeo and Juliet*—The fight scene Act 3, Scene 1, lines 61–111

The teacher, Melanie Watts, a high school teacher from Powys, began by giving the students one minute with talk partners to discuss this question: "What does the director of a play or film do?" Answers were collected.

They then watched a short video clip of the fight scene. Students were encouraged to note facial expressions, movements, tone of voice, etc.

Two Answers A and B from students from last year's class were projected, and students were given discussion time to decide which was better and why.

Tybalt: Romeo, the love I bear thee can afford
        No better term that this-thou art a villain.

How to direct an actor -
Which piece of writing is better and why?

A. In this part of the scene Tybalt finally comes face to face with Romeo. This is the moment he has been waiting for since the Capulet party. He is furious and desperate to fight Romeo. Tybalt tries to start a fight by insulting him and by calling him a "villain".

B. Tybalt is still very angry because Romeo went to the Capulet party so he must pause before he says the words "thou art a villain". The words need to be said quietly so that only Romeo can hear but also slowly and deliberately with the greatest emphasis on the word "villain". Tybalt can stand very close to Romeo to make him feel threatened and uncomfortable. Tybalt's face needs to have a grim and determined look.

The students gave their response, generating the success criteria while doing so. The teacher annotated the "best" piece as directed by the students. The final success criteria, in the students' own words, follow.

how he is feeling   why he is feeling this way
Tybalt is still very angry because Romeo went to
                              where to pause
the Capulet party so he must pause before he

says the words "thou art a villain". The words
              how to speak the lines
need to be said quietly so that only Romeo can
              how to speak the lines
hear but also slowly and deliberately with the
how to speak the lines
greatest emphasis on the word "villain". Tybalt
        movements and actions
can stand very close to Romeo to make him feel

threatened and uncomfortable. Tybalt's face
        facial expression
needs to have a grim and determined look.

(Continued)

(Continued)

Director's Notes Success Criteria

Give advice to the actor on the following:

- The way that they need to say their lines (e.g., shouting, whispering, knowing where to pause)
- Facial expressions
- The tone of voice that they need to use
- The movements and actions they should make and why
- What they are thinking and feeling and why

Students then discussed their task, ready for the next lesson, in which they wrote their own directors' notes, peer assessed them against the success criteria, and developed them further.

Melanie: "The impact of this approach on their work was quite pronounced as the quality of the work was so much better and much more focused—they did actually understand that they needed to 'tell' the actors how to act out the scene. Also, while they were actually producing the work, there was less fussing and complaints of 'I don't know how to do this.'"

Melanie Watts, Learning Leader, Crickhowell High School, Powys

Further Examples of Good vs. Poor as a Basis for Co-Construction

A balanced argument vs. a biased argument

A correctly set out line graph vs. uneven axes and incorrect plotting

A correct sentence in French vs. an incorrect sentence in French

Clear instructions for making something vs. very unclear instructions

And so on!

Video 6.1: Watch Hannah and her TA co-construct the success criteria for self-portraits with four- and five-year-olds.

Strategy 3: Demonstrate the Steps at the Front of the Room

1. Using a visualizer or document camera, tell the students to watch what you do while you demonstrate a skill in action or some writing or mathematics. Do this silently.

2. Stop after the first step and ask, "What did I just do?" Take their responses, and write this up as the first success criterion.

3. Continue in this way until all success criteria are written up at the front. Older students might find it useful to write these in their own books as you write them up.

Video 6.2: Watch Sarah with sixteen-year-olds co-constructing the success criteria for a good written method in a science experiment.

A smart board or document camera will allow you to project anything to the front of the room and still allow you to face the class as you are writing or drawing. One effective use of these tools is to demonstrate how to do something, using the document camera; stopping at each point; asking, "What did I do first?," "What did I do next?"; taking their responses; and writing up the criteria as you go. Use this strategy for any skill that has different ingredients or techniques, as in the following examples:

> Demonstrating how to use a particular art tool (e.g., inks or watercolors), where you keep stopping to gather the criteria about how to hold the brush, how to mix colors, how much of the medium to use at a time, etc.
>
> Demonstrating how to look up some information for an information retrieval learning intention (where to start, use of indexes, or internet searches and what to do)
>
> Demonstrating how to use a dictionary
>
> Demonstrating how to draw a line graph
>
> And so on . . .

Strategy 4: Demonstrate How *Not* to Do Something at the Front of the Room (Play the Fool)

1. Tell the students that you are going to show them how to . . . (choose a skill that you think they might already know something about).

2. Start and talk as you are demonstrating something, making the steps very deliberate, either at the visualizer or document camera or in front of the class if it is something requiring more space to demonstrate (e.g., a science experiment).

3. It might take a couple of seconds, but the class should start laughing or calling out (young children will shout indignantly that you are doing it wrong).

4. Ask, innocently, what you did wrong, affect surprise, and write up what you should have done first (as the first success criterion).

5. Continue doing everything wrong. The students will realize what's happening and will enjoy correcting you! Each correct success criterion is written up as you go.

When you think students have a little knowledge about something, playing at not being able to do something correctly sends them into calling out what you're doing wrong and what you should be doing instead. Obviously, this would be inappropriate for a skill that students would have had no experience with, so it works well to consolidate previous learning and is fun to use with young students.

EXAMPLE 6.3: Using Strategy 4 to Demonstrate How *Not* to Count Properly With Young Students

Demonstrating with four- and five-year-olds how not to count properly (overcounting first until they tell you how to organize the cubes so that you can count them more easily; then not moving the counters as you count so that you still don't know which ones you've counted; then going back to the beginning again rather than stopping at the last one). You should end up with these criteria, with helpful pictures beside them, through correction by the class:

- Put them in a line.
- Count every single cube.
- Move each one as you count.
- The last one in the line is the total in the group.

Video 6.3: Watch Hannah with four- and five-year-olds co-constructing the success criteria for how to count.

The following examples are also suitable for demonstrating how not to do it, with students correcting you at each step. They have to phrase the success criteria so that it makes sense, so this strategy is very useful for developing language fluency:

How to put on a coat

How to form letters

How to use scissors correctly

How to tidy up the role-play area

With older students, this strategy is useful to see how much they know or can do for a skill or knowledge, which you think they are reasonably confident with. Start writing some wrong facts mixed with correct facts, start drawing a map or diagram that is wrong, start demonstrating how to draw a particular angle or shape with some wrong properties being labeled, etc. The students enjoy correcting you, of course!

Strategy 5: Finding the Mistake

1. Show the class an example of any procedure that has definite, chronological steps (such as a mathematics calculation).

2. Ask if students can find the error (they will have to check every step so the co-construction of the success criteria becomes clear).

3. Together, compile the steps that form the success criteria.

Students love to find mistakes, given an example with an error. You can make up something yourself or use an anonymous example of a math calculation from a student's work from a previous year.

Look at these examples, and try to spot the mistake yourself:

Spot the Mistake!	Spot the Mistake!
For a lesson on partitioning numbers to multiply:	**For a lesson on multiplication grids:**
$18 \times 5 = ?$	How many sweets altogether?
$10 \times 5 = 50$ $8 \times 5 = 45$	26, 26, 26, 26, 26, 26, 26
$50 + 45 = 95$	<table><tr><td>x</td><td>20</td><td>7</td></tr><tr><td>6</td><td>120</td><td>42</td></tr></table>
$18 \times 5 = 95$	$120 + 42 = 162$
	$26 \times 7 = 162$

In the first example, a mistake was made when multiplying 8×5. In the second example, the table was set up to multiply 27×6 instead of 26×7.

Notice that you have to start from the beginning and check every step to ensure accuracy. This means that you can ask students, after they've found the mistake, what you do first, what is next, and so on, writing these success criteria as you go on a whiteboard or flip chart or anything that can be displayed in the room for the next few days as a reference for students.

Strategy 6: Mixing Up the Success Criteria

1. Show the students a good finished product.

2. Have prewritten success criteria on cards in a bag.

3. Take them out, and display the criteria in a random order.

4. Ask the students to first discuss in pairs the correct order to fit the finished product.

This strategy works well for a mathematics skill or science experiment and creates good discussion.

It can also be effective to include some "rogue" success criteria, which shouldn't be included at all! For younger children, make these very obvious, but as we go up the age range, make the rogue criteria less obvious to encourage more debate.

Strategy 7: Eavesdropping

1. Present students with the learning intention.

2. Ask them to talk with a learning partner for a minute or two to list all the necessary steps.

3. Walk around the room, jotting down what you hear.

4. Reveal the list of success criteria they came up with after the discussion time is up.

This strategy works well when the learning intention of the lesson is something that you believe the students will probably already know quite a lot about. If they have missed out on any elements, don't be worried about adding your own ideas—it is co-constructing after all.

Here are some examples of learning intentions suitable for eavesdropping:

- To write a newspaper article

- To write an invitation

- To write instructions

- To write an informal letter

- To write persuasively

- To know properties of 3D shapes

- To know the different lines of symmetry

Video 6.4: Watch Denise with seven-year-olds eavesdropping to co-construct the success criteria for a newspaper article.

For older students, this strategy can be used for retrieval practice for learning intentions that you know they will have covered in previous years.

Even with this quick strategy, however, we need to remember that analyzing what a good one looks like (WAGOLL), and often a poor example too, takes students' understanding to a higher level. So, after gathering the ingredients of an invitation, for instance, the next step would be to *look at two examples of invitations—one with missing information and one complete.*

To take this further, *show them two invitations that have all the success criteria fulfilled, but one is better than the other.* Their analysis will bring out what excellence looks like, going beyond the success criteria.

Examples of Co-Constructed Success Criteria Across All Ages and Subjects

Part 4 will detail how to plan and develop learning intentions and success criteria in each subject area, but the following list offers a quick example of co-constructed success criteria in each age range.

Four- and Five-Year-Olds: Writing Example

Top Tips—Let's Get Ready to Write

- Use the hand that feels the comfiest.
- You need to sit on the chair properly.
- Put your thumb underneath the pencil and the first finger on the top.
- Hold the paper with your other hand or it might move.

Six- and Seven-Year-Olds: Mathematics Example

Learning intention: To add two-digit numbers on a number line (e.g., 34 + 58)

Remember to:
- Find the biggest number on the number line (58).
- Look at the next number, and jump the tens first (34 has three tens so 68, 78, 88).
- Now jump the units (four units left so 89, 90, 91, 92).
- The last number you land on is the total of the two numbers (92).

Eight- to Ten-Year-Olds: Writing Example

Learning intention: To write a story opening for a scary story (eight- and nine-year-olds having discussed a good and a not-so-good example)

Choose to include:
- A flashback
- Dialogue
- A description
- A significant event
- Your own idea

Eight- to Ten-Year-Olds: Mathematics Example

Learning intention: To solve word problems (eight- and nine-year-olds analyzing three excellent examples of solved problems and what they had in common)

Choose from:
- Highlighting key words
- Drawing a diagram
- Using symbols
- Making a chart

Eleven- and Twelve-Year-Olds: Art Example

Learning intention: To create a collage

Remember to:
- Stick materials on the paper.
- Cover most of the paper.
- Choose colors, materials, and design.
- Make it eye catching.

Fourteen-Year-Olds: Writing Example

Learning intention: To write a play script

- Character's name written in the margin to show who is speaking
- Stage directions written inside brackets [ ] ( ) { }
- Each speech written on a new line
- No speech marks
- No use of the word *said*
- Stage directions to describe the setting
- Stage directions to tell the actor how to say their speech and what to do on stage
- Use of adverbs and adjectives in stage directions

Age Seventeen: Mathematics Example

Learning intention: To solve a quadratic equation with real roots, using the quadratic formula

Remember to Put equation in $ax^2 + bx + c = 0$ form.

- Identify the values of a, b, c.
- Substitute values into quadratic formula.
- Simplify.
- Express roots appropriately.
- Consider a method to check your solutions.

What Happens to the Co-Constructed Success Criteria?

Teachers, sometimes with the help of a TA, usually write the success criteria on the smart board via a laptop or on a flip chart or whiteboard as they are being co-constructed. The students then refer to these during the lesson.

Some teachers ask students to copy the criteria into their books, but this is unnecessary as long as the criteria are in the room and visible. With writing tasks, having the criteria in their books can make students think that if they've ticked them off or checked them, then they have achieved the task. With open learning intentions, simply including the criteria ("I've included two similes!") is no guarantee of the quality of the finished product.

I have seen schools where the frequently used success criteria, after co-construction, are written on cards that the students keep so that they can easily retrieve them. I remember one teacher saying that, after a while, he noticed that the students no longer took out the cards as they had internalized and remembered them. How powerful! Imaging moving up to your next school already knowing what you need to include in a number of skills. . . .

I have also seen schools in which mastery mathematics schemes are used, asking students to provide a written narrative for the steps in a calculation, so the criteria are self-created.

The advantage of typing the criteria into a laptop or any device that can save the criteria is that they can be easily retrieved for another lesson that needs the same criteria.

An important point is that each new class will need to co-construct the success criteria to maximize their impact, even though you have last year's version at hand.

Many transferable skills are used throughout the school, with the co-constructed success criteria becoming more and more sophisticated as the students get older. The success criteria for seven-year-olds writing a newspaper article, for instance, would be much more basic (headline, subheading, pictures, etc.) than the same for sixteen-year-olds, who might be thinking about the tone of an article, any emotive or inflammatory language used, and so on.

The Impact of Co-Constructed Process Success Criteria

The Impact for Students

- Students have more ownership of their work—they are generating their own success criteria so it is more relevant to them—rather than being teacher directed.

- It raises self-efficacy; they set the targets (i.e., success criteria) and get positive feedback when they self-assess and see that their work satisfies the criteria.

- Students are more confident, and the quality of work has improved—more revisions and self-regulation.

- They remember their input and refer to the success criteria when working.

- Seeing students' previous excellent work inspires them, but also they want to do "better."

- Success criteria provide a platform for both self- and peer assessments.

- Students become more reflective thinkers and become more critical thinkers—analytical skills being developed.

- Students become more independent and self-reliant.

- Differentiation is addressed: once success criteria have been formulated, lower achievers might focus on two or three key criteria, and the teacher's role is to make sure all students have access to the success criteria.

- Students have appropriate focus criteria while engaged in the task.

- The criteria can be used as a focus for self-assessment, available for self-monitoring while engaged in the activity and afterward (Where am I achieving success? Where do I need to indicate that I need some help?).

- The success criteria form the feedback criteria for peer evaluation.

- Success criteria help students develop a sense of what is and what is not important—vital for future independent learning.

The Impact for Teacher

- Planning time is often cut by approximately 50 percent, because success criteria essentially provide the lesson agenda. The activity details in the plan can, as a consequence, be abbreviated. Concerns about resourcing and modeling the focus points become more important than simply listing the tasks that will take place during the lesson. Overplanning the activity leads to a straitjacketing effect, where the success of a lesson can be mistakenly attributed to having gotten through all the planned tasks. The only thing that matters is whether learning is taking place in the lesson according to the learning intention.

- The planned activity is more likely to match and therefore fulfill the learning objective.

- Feedback to students is automatically focused around the success criteria, resulting in more specific and accurate targeting of needs.

SUMMARY OF KEY POINTS

1. Co-constructed success criteria are more clearly owned, understood, and remembered by students than simply being given.

2. If the co-constructed strategy involved analyzing good examples, students have the added bonus of knowing more explicitly what excellence could consist of.

3. There are at least seven efficient, effective co-construction strategies for gathering process success criteria:

   - Identifying features of two or three examples
   - Comparing good and poor examples
   - Demonstrating and stopping at each step
   - Demonstrating how not to do something
   - Mixing up success criteria or including rogue success criteria
   - Eavesdropping

4. Write the success criteria up at the front as they are co-constructed so that students have them to refer to during the task.

Planning a Lesson 7

The following tables and examples might help clarify the different terms used throughout the book so far before we look at possible pathways for planning a lesson or series of lessons. The first table gives the terminology and the second gives examples of those:

EXAMPLE 7.1: Basic Terminology Used in This Book for Learning Intentions and Success Criteria

What does the curriculum consist of?	Taught specifics (surface stage)	Applications (how students apply their learning—deep)
How do they break down into learning intentions?	Closed skills (to know how to . . .) Knowledge (to know that . . .)	Open skills (to know how to . . .) Usually linked with the context knowledge learning intention
What are the implications for success criteria?	Closed skills need compulsory rules to achieve mastery. Knowledge needs access to prompts, materials, or key focus points—no success criteria.	Open skills need a menu or toolkit of suggested strategies or inclusions. Knowledge needs access to prompts, materials, or key focus points—no success criteria.

EXAMPLE 7.2: Examples to Illustrate Example 7.1

WHAT DOES THE CURRICULUM CONSIST OF?	TAUGHT SPECIFICS (SURFACE STAGE)	APPLICATIONS (HOW STUDENTS APPLY THEIR LEARNING—DEEP)
How do they break into learning intentions?	**Closed skills:** a. To calculate the angles of a triangle b. To use scissors correctly c. To use commas correctly **Knowledge:** To know the reasons for the Cold War	**Open skills:** a. To write a description **Context:** Rain b. To solve a mathematics word problem **Knowledge link:** Using all four operations c. To design a tourist leaflet **Knowledge link:** To know about Paris
What are the implications for success criteria?	Closed skills have compulsory rules to achieve mastery. **For example:** After co-construction for *a*: **Remember to:** Use your protractor to measure each angle. • Make sure they total 180 degrees. • If two angles are given, total these and subtract the total from 180 degrees to get the missing angle Knowledge has key focus points or access to a textbook or other materials.	Open skills have a list of suggested strategies or inclusions but are not compulsory unless indicated by the teacher. **For example:** After co-construction for *a*: **Choose from:** • Adjectives (use words instead of *wet!*) • Similes • Alliteration (if it sounds good) • A setting that helps the reader imagine • Etc. **After co-construction for *c*:** Two columns—One for the elements of a tourist leaflet (transferable skill) and the other for key facts to remember about Paris
What are the implications for quality?	Demonstration, practice, and seeing what a good one looks like (WAGOLL) help to develop student expertise.	Open skills (applications) need whole-class analysis of at least two excellent anonymous examples and/or comparison

WHAT DOES THE CURRICULUM CONSIST OF?	TAUGHT SPECIFICS (SURFACE STAGE)	APPLICATIONS (HOW STUDENTS APPLY THEIR LEARNING—DEEP)
	Once the skill has been mastered, there is no quality difference between students. Knowledge points rely on students' ability to access it when needed and memorize it if tested.	of excellent with poor. This establishes success criteria but gives understanding of WAGOLL in practice. Where there is a knowledge link, as in c, it would be important to look at, for example, a tourist leaflet in which all the elements of a tourist leaflet are included but the knowledge of Paris is poor. Knowledge must be given equal status to the skill to avoid either being neglected.
What language is best used in displaying the success criteria?	Use "Remember to . . ."	Use "Choose from . . ." Unless the skill is for nonfiction writing, use "Remember to . . ." for the structural success criteria.

Now that I know all about learning intentions and success criteria, how do I start planning a lesson?

Follow the Path for Skills, Knowledge, or Both

FIGURE 7.1 Pathway for Planning a Lesson for Learning Intentions and Success Criteria

Planning Process A: Planning for Skills

1. Plan the success criteria (What do they have to do? Are there any rules or definitions?).

2. Decide which strategy to use to co-construct the success criteria.

3. Show one excellent example (from a previous class) to analyze against the success criteria (Have they achieved the success criteria?) or, if in written form, show a good one next to a poor example and have a class discussion about why one is better than the other (this could be your co-constructing strategy).

4. Students do their independent work against the success criteria and with some understanding of what excellence looks like.

SUCCESS DEPENDS ON GETTING THE ANSWERS RIGHT OR, IN WRITING, INCLUDING THE RELEVANT INFORMATION.

(Continued)

(Continued)

Planning Process B: Planning for Knowledge

1. The learning intention is only needed if there is to be no application of the knowledge. The lesson would consist of teaching or instruction and/or using resources, exploration, investigation, and discussion. No success criteria are needed until the knowledge is applied in some way.

SUCCESS IS NOT QUANTIFIABLE UNTIL THE APPLICATION STAGE.

Planning Process C: Planning for Both Skills and Knowledge

1. Decide whether the children need to co-construct success criteria for the generic skill. It might have been used before—in which case just bring up the success criteria from a previous lesson. If it is new, do 1, 2, and 3 from Planning Process A.

2. The knowledge link needs equal status to the skill, so decide which elements of the knowledge you want them to focus on, and list those next to the skill success criteria.

SUCCESS DEPENDS ON ACHIEVING BOTH THE SKILL AND INCLUDING THE KEY KNOWELDGE INFORMATION.

How Do Learning Intentions and Success Criteria Work in the Flow of a Lesson?

Learning intentions are only one aspect of formative assessment. My last two books outline all aspects of formative assessment, but as this book is devoted to only this aspect, the following example shows how learning intentions are embedded into the flow of a lesson. Look for the boldface phrases to see where learning intentions and success criteria fit into the full planning process.

EXAMPLE 7.3: Learning Intentions Embedded in the Flow of a Typical Lesson

---

Before lesson

- **Learning intentions for lessons planned in the short term**
- **Success criteria thought about by the teacher**
- Good and not so good anonymous examples of finished products sourced (e.g., written work, artwork, 3D objects, photographs of things too bulky to store, video clips of PE or games skills, video clips of drama). Use internet resources, make them up yourself, or use scanned copies of student work from previous years.

Lesson

- The teacher briefly refers to whole unit coverage, stating what learning has taken place so far, where it is now, and what is still to come for this unit of work.
- A good formative question is asked for the first five minutes, which will get the students **thinking and discussing the subject matter of the learning intention** in talk partners, their responses revealing their understanding and misconceptions. **The learning intention is then revealed.**

- The two examples of contrasting previous work are projected or shared with the class visually for initial class analysis with talk partners to do the following:

  1. **Determine success criteria** (What can you see?) and for open skills only.

  2. **Identify quality through comparing the two pieces against those success criteria** (Why is this sentence or aspect better than this one?).

- Students' work takes place, with **continual checking against the success criteria.**

- Once, twice, or more, a random student's work is projected at the front, there and then, and students, in pairs, analyze it for success and improvement needs, suggesting actual improvements that are then made as a class.

- Using this as a model, the students **then identify success and make improvements** in their own work via self or paired discussions.

- The lesson ends with summary of learning, examples of improvements made, and reference to the next learning focus.

SUMMARY OF KEY POINTS

1. Follow the pathways when planning a lesson, as knowing whether the learning intention(s) for the lesson are skills, knowledge, or knowledge applied via a skill affect how the lesson is taught and how the success criteria are evolved and used.

2. The possible lesson flow incorporates learning intentions in a lesson in which formative assessment strategies are used, such as a starter prior knowledge question, talk partner discussions, ongoing feedback, and class analysis of students' work mid-lesson to help all students in the room see examples of excellence and go through the process of making ongoing improvements.

Differences Between Subjects

Literacy

Writing

8

It would be so much easier if every subject conformed to a generic pattern for success criteria, and, apart from writing, on the whole, it does. I start this section with literacy writing, used in almost all subjects in order to discuss the important issue of quality and knowing what excellence looks like, which is the guiding instructional point for this subject. I then move on to other subjects where the issues are simpler.

Planning Graphic for Writing

The following graphic (Example 8.1) shows the planning steps or route for the three different elements of writing (nonfiction; fiction; and grammar, spelling, and punctuation [secretarial skills in the UK]) and some suggested posters.

EXAMPLE 8.1: Planning Pathway for an English Lesson in Which Students Have to Write

Nonfiction	Fiction
Identify transferable skill learning intention and linked knowledge learning intention (e.g., **Learning intention:** To analyze poetry, giving evidence of claims and	**Identify skill learning intention and context** (e.g., **Learning intention:** To write using effects that create suspense and

(Continued)

(Continued)

Learning intention: Walt Whitman's themes in his poems and how they mirror the primary values of America's founding)

Decide the success criteria for the transferable skill:

Remember to:

- State the purpose at the beginning.
- Write about each theme in the poems in turn.
- Use quotes to illustrate your points.
- Point out poetry techniques and how they enhance the poem.
- Give some personal opinions.
- Include author's intent and impact on the reader.

Decide the key points or success criteria for the knowledge.

Plan how to co-construct the success criteria for the skill (e.g., identify why this poetry analysis from last year's class is better than this one)

SUCCESS depends on knowing what excellence looks like, using the skill success criteria and including the appropriate knowledge, but it is subjective.

Context: A starting point of "Joanne stood alone in the dark. She could hear something scratching. . . .")

Decide optional toolkit success criteria for the skill:

- Main character(s) alone
- Setting is threatening
- Threat is unnamed
- Short sentences
- Ellipsis
- Threatening verbs

Plan how to co-construct the success criteria (e.g., given three excellent short pieces of suspense, identify what features the author has used to create suspense)

SUCCESS depends on knowing what excellence looks like, choosing from the success criteria, but it is subjective.

Punctuation, grammar, handwriting, spelling

Identify skill learning intention (e.g., using similes)

Decide success criteria:

- Compare something to something else.
- Use the connectives *like* or *as ____ as*).
- Etc.

Plan how to co-construct the success criteria (e.g., show some phrases that are similes and some that are not, and ask what makes the difference).

SUCCESS is guaranteed if success criteria are met.

Posters: Reminders for all writing (everlasting success criteria) to keep on display permanently.

Every time we write . . .

Writing techniques . . .

(see the examples of these on p. 66)

Skills—Open or Closed

Writing learning intentions tend to be either *open or closed skills*. It is only important to know this because of the impact on success criteria, feedback, and quality.

> *Closed skill learning intentions,* as in grammar, punctuation, and spelling, always have compulsory elements for the learning intention to be fulfilled (e.g., every rule must be obeyed in speech punctuation for attainment). If the success criteria have been achieved, with accuracy, the learning intention will be achieved. The success criteria for closed learning intentions are often known as *rules.*

> *Open skill learning intentions* (e.g., most writing, whether nonfiction [to write a persuasive argument, to write a newspaper article, or to write up an account of a historical event] or fiction [to create a characterization or to create suspense in writing]) can only give structural points or suggestions of authors' techniques. Although helpful, these do not guarantee quality—success in writing is dependent upon the impact on the reader; success in composing a piece of music depends on the impact on the listener; success in art depends upon the impact on the observer. Analyzing excellent examples and comparing with poor examples, however, help students develop an understanding of what excellence looks like and how it is achieved. The success criteria for open learning intentions are often known as *tools.*

EXAMPLE 8.2: The Difference Between Closed Skills (Compulsory Success Criteria) and Open Skills (Optional Success Criteria) in Writing

Closed rules skill (compulsory ingredients): Once mastered, the learning intention is achieved.	**Open toolkit skill (menu of possibilities):** Success criteria don't guarantee quality; they give suggestions of what could be included.
Learning intention: To use apostrophes correctly (twelve-year-olds and higher!)	**Learning intention:** To write a story opening (nine-year-olds)
Remember to use apostrophes . . .	**Choose all or some:**

Closed (left column, continued):

Remember to use apostrophes . . .

- For possession singular (e.g., My brother's dog—one brother)
- When the plural has no s on the end (e.g., children's dog/men's dog/people's church)
- For possession plural (e.g., my brothers' dog—many brothers)
- For contractions (e.g., *don't* for *do not, isn't* for *is not*)
- **Remember!** Don't put an apostrophe in *its* when used for possession (e.g., She watched the sea and heard its crashing waves.).

Open (right column, continued):

Choose all or some:

- **Setting:** e.g., dialogue or description, introduction of characters, introduction of problem
- Hook the reader: Show not tell; suggest what might happen or have happened.
- Use senses.
- Create powerful images for the reader.
- Use our "what makes good writing" success list.

Examples of Literacy Skills With Knowledge Links

To add to the examples already given in the preceding chapters, more examples of English literacy success criteria for skills and the linking knowledge now follow, with the skills success criteria co-constructed with students.

EXAMPLE 8.3: Skill Learning Intentions and Their Success Criteria Linked With Context Knowledge Key Points

SKILL LEARNING INTENTION WE ARE LEARNING . . .	SUCCESS CRITERIA (WHAT YOU NEED TO DO TO ACHIEVE THE LEARNING INTENTION) *These are planned, determine the instruction of the lesson, and are co-constructed with the students and written up just before they start to work.*	KNOWLEDGE LEARNING INTENTION TO KNOW . . .	KEY POINTS NEEDED TO APPLY IN THE SKILL
To use complex sentences (elementary/ primary)	**Remember to:** <ul><li>Use appropriate connectives.</li><li>Include main and subordinate clauses.</li><li>Vary the position of the subclause for effect.</li></ul>	*The Jungle Book,* first chapter	<ul><li>Use correct names: Baloo, Bagheera, Mowgli, Shere Khan</li><li>Shere Khan's argument to get rid of Mowgli</li><li>Mother and Father Wolf's responses</li></ul>
To be able to write instructions (elementary/ primary)	**Remember to:** <ul><li>Write everything in the correct order.</li><li>Use bullet points; numbers; or first, second, etc.</li><li>Use imperatives (bossy verbs).</li><li>Include adverbs if they clarify the instruction.</li><li>Use your scaffold sheet.</li></ul>	How to make Jell-O	<ul><li>Include choice of flavors.</li><li>Decide whether or not to add fruit.</li><li>Think about different shapes and containers.</li></ul>
To write persuasively using different techniques (elementary/middle/ lower secondary)	**Remember to include:** <ul><li>A statement of your viewpoint</li><li>A number of reasons for this with evidence</li><li>A number of reasons from an alternative standpoint</li></ul>	About the Common Council of our city to hire more lifeguards to keep municipal swimming pools open for longer in the summer	**Consider:** <ul><li>Funding</li><li>Training of lifeguards</li><li>Number of pools</li></ul>

SKILL LEARNING INTENTION ⇨ WE ARE LEARNING . . .	SUCCESS CRITERIA (WHAT YOU NEED TO DO TO ACHIEVE THE LEARNING INTENTION) *These are planned, determine the instruction of the lesson, and are co-constructed with the students and written up just before they start to work.*	KNOWLEDGE LEARNING INTENTION ⇨ TO KNOW . . .	KEY POINTS NEEDED TO APPLY IN THE SKILL
	• Attempts at striking up empathy with the recipient • Recommended alternative action • A summary • Reasoning connectives		• Other staffing factors • Average attendance
To know and use a variety of spelling strategies (primary/ elementary)	**Remember to:** • Use a rule that you already know. • Think of other words with the same spelling pattern. • Look for smaller words within the word. • Look at the word carefully. Does it look right? • Count the syllables. • Sound it out. • Use mnemonics.	ABCD Word Game (multiple choice)	No key points
To work out meanings of unknown words (elementary)	**Remember to:** • Take clues from the context. • Look at the roots of words. • Look for patterns or combinations. • Look for a prefix or suffix. • Look for assonance/ onomatopoeia.	"The Pied Piper of Hamelin" poem by Robert Browning	No key points
To compare two poems (high/upper secondary)	**Remember to:** • Analyze the poems first. • Annotate for meaning and features (similes, onomatopoeia, iambic pentameter, etc.).	"Tissue" by Imtiaz Dharker and "My Last Duchess" by Robert Browning	See background information on the setting for the Browning poem, and see YouTube for Dharker's inspiration for the poem.

(Continued)

(Continued)

SKILL LEARNING INTENTION ⇨ WE ARE LEARNING . . .	SUCCESS CRITERIA (WHAT YOU NEED TO DO TO ACHIEVE THE LEARNING INTENTION) *These are planned, determine the instruction of the lesson, and are co-constructed with the students and written up just before they start to work.*	KNOWLEDGE LEARNING INTENTION ⇨ TO KNOW . . .	KEY POINTS NEEDED TO APPLY IN THE SKILL
	• Choose three or four key ideas that link the poems. • Compare using connectives (similarly, to contrast, etc.). • Give evidence to support your claims (because . . . and quotes). • Focus on the author's intent and the impact on the reader.		
How character development impacts plot (high/upper secondary)	**Remember to include:** • List the main changes in the character's development in chronological order (a character arc?). • For each key change, give examples and specific quotes to illustrate these. • Describe how the key changes impact what happens in the plot (cause and effect). • Use quotes to show other characters' changing opinions in light of the character's development. • Use evidence from the story to back up your claims.	The character of Mr. Darcy in *Pride and Prejudice*	**Consider:** • Darcy's first appearance and how he is judged (Does he really change after this, or has he been misjudged?) • The role of gossip in people's beliefs about Darcy • Darcy's personality • The impact of Elizabeth's words on his behavior • The impact of pride, honor, and prejudice in Darcy's life • The impact of other people's influence on Darcy
To create an effective tourist leaflet (middle/lower secondary)	**Remember to include:** • Summary information • Clear headlines • Key tourist spots • Pictures • Places, accommodations • Sightseeing highlights, food, leisure	About tourism in Paris	**Consider:** • French cuisine • Eiffel Tower and other famous sights • The Seine river • Galleries (Musée d'Orsay, Louvre, etc.) • Range of accommodation

Breaking Down Success Criteria for Closer Focus

Broad key skills produce broad success criteria, so it can often be necessary to take each of the success criteria in turn and make those the focus of a lesson or series of lessons. *Persuasive writing* would be a good example of this, where each element is worthy of a number of lessons.

EXAMPLE 8.4: A Skill Learning Intention With Success Criteria—Each Worthy of a Lesson

To write a persuasive argument	Letter to local senator/MP	• A statement of your viewpoint
		• A number of reasons for this with evidence
		• A number of reasons from an alternative standpoint
		• Attempts at striking up empathy with the recipient
		• Recommended alternative action
		• A summary
		• Reasoning connectives

We could take "striking up empathy," for instance, present pupils with two contrasting examples of persuasive letters—one that empathizes well and one that doesn't—and get them to analyze the pieces in order to generate success criteria for empathy.

EXAMPLE 8.5: One of the Persuasive Writing Success Criteria Broken Into Further Success Criteria

To express empathy in an argument	Letter to local senator/MP	• Flattery
		• Mentioning something personal to the recipient
		• Appealing to his or her better nature

The Critical Issue of Quality and Knowing What Good Examples Look Like

Any successful prose writing, for students of any age, depends not only on the learning intention, success criteria, and good instruction. It also depends on how well the student has written. Writing begins in reading, so you will have noticed how the avid readers in your class or school are almost certainly the best writers. This is because, in order to write well, children have to read widely, deeply, and regularly so that the rhythms and patterns of effective prose become part of their linguistic bank—and so that their imaginative world is deepened and broadened. Reading is the writer's yardstick.

One of the most effective mantras to help student writing is to emphasize the author's intent and the impact on the reader: What do you want your reader to think and feel? I have seen many posters in classrooms with lists of "what makes good writing" criteria, containing writing techniques: adjectives, adverbs, personification, similes, metaphors, and so on. These are tools, but more is needed. Perhaps the elements included in Example 8.6 would be more effective as a writing guide—clearly age related. Clichéd descriptions in young children's writing are welcomed, as are any adjectives, whereas older students need to be shown how overwriting (too many adjectives) can spoil the impact and obvious settings (e.g., haunted house for a ghost story) should be avoided.

EXAMPLE 8.6: Everlasting Success Criteria for "What Makes Good Writing"

> **What makes good writing (for any genre)**
> - What effect do you want your opening to have on the reader?
> - What will do this best (e.g., dialogue/flashback/descriptive setting/significant event)?
> - Have you avoided obvious or clichéd descriptions in your writing?
> - Have you made sure your adjectives tell the reader something they would not have known?
> - Have you chosen interesting, informative nouns and verbs (e.g., "the policeman stared at the golden eagle" rather than "the man looked at the bird")?
> - Have you *shown* the reader how characters feel or look, rather than *telling* them?
> - Does your writing make the reader want to read on?
> - How do you want the reader to feel when they read your ending? Choose the best way of doing this.

Comparing Good and Poor Examples

Because many children are not avid readers, we need to do more to help them develop their understanding of what excellence looks like by exposing them to many examples of excellent text, ranging from published texts to short examples of writing from previous students in our school. One of the best resources a teacher can have is to have saved two or three excellent products and one mediocre example for every lesson in which a product is written by students. These can then be used for future lessons, anonymously, for students to analyze as a class and see and hear what good writing does and does not look and sound like, depending on the author's intent, of course.

EXAMPLE 8.7: Contrasting Examples of an Advertisement

Advertisement A

THE AMAZING LIFE-SIZED ROBOT!

VOTED ONE OF THE BEST TOYS

WE HAVE PLENTY IN STOCK!

Children, are you looking for a best friend? A toy, that does more than any other toy ever seen before? A toy that you have only seen in your dreams?

Well look no further, help is here with the incredible, ROCKY ROBOT here just for YOU!

The ROCKY ROBOT is like no other robot that has ever been made before!

This toy for YOU; it will be a superb, special and sensational addition to YOUR toy collection and it will help you with your chores!

The ROCKY ROBOT has many breakthrough and exclusive benefits including:

- It can help with all your chores such as cleaning your room, washing the dishes and can even do your homework!
- Special sensors mean that your robot will never crash into anything and last forever!
- This incredible robot can speak 25 different languages.
- Its special features include a DVD player, USB dock, mobile phone and it can even connect to the internet.

So what are you waiting for? Let the Marvellous, ROCKY ROBOT in your toy box today and you'll have the privilege of owning the most mind-blowing Robot- EVER!

HAVE A ROCKING TIME WITH ROCKY ROBOT!

'This is the best thing I have ever bought! I play with it every day and never get bored. If you haven't got one . . . get one now!'

Callum, Aged 10

Compared to:

Advertisement B

THE AMAZING LIFE-SIZED ROBOT!

HURRY! WHILE STOCKS LAST!

VOTED BEST TOY OF 2021!

Children, are you looking for a good toy?

The ROCKY ROBOT is great!

The ROCKY ROBOT the following benefits:

- It is grey
- It takes batteries and can move
- It has a great remote control.

BUY 25 AND GET 1 FREE!

'This is a nice toy'
Callum, Aged 10

ROCKY ROBOT IS FUN. IT IS A TOY YOU SHOULD DEFINITELY HAVE AND ONE YOU WILL LOVE. SO HURRY UP AND COME AND BUY IT!

Langford Primary School

95

The issue of knowing what a good one looks like (WAGOLL), or preferably seeing what more than one good example looks like to increase student knowledge of excellence, is critical for learning intentions and success criteria to have meaning for nonfiction and fiction writing.

Example 8.7 shows good and bad examples of persuasive advertisements created by Seamus Gibbons from Langford School. Students (aged nine) were asked to compare the two as the vehicle for then co-constructing the success criteria for a persuasive advertisement. They then started to write their own persuasive advertisements for a different product.

I observed this lesson, and not only did the students find the lesson engaging and amusing but they confidently co-constructed the success criteria for a persuasive advertisement and, in doing so, had first-hand experience of what a good one might look like.

How to Compare and Analyze Contrasting Examples of the Previous Class's Writing

Video 8.1: Watch Julie with eleven-year-olds co-constructing criteria for a written description of the graphic novel *The Arrival*, by Shaun Tan.

As discussed in Chapters 5 and 6, the process of whole-class analysis of good examples is critical to students understanding what quality might look like. Comparing good with poor examples is also effective, as students see what is considered excellence and what is not. With older students, it is also useful to compare, as a class, an excellent piece with a good piece. Both of the extracts in Example 8.8 are good, but one is better than the other. The subtle differences between them encourage deep levels of analysis.

Good and not so good examples of writing (always anonymous) can be highlighted across similar elements, as in the example that follows, so that specific comparisons can be made, as in the following texts, with questions that aim to help students talk about good writing beyond the technical features. I have included possible questions a teacher might ask talk partners to discuss. Notice that technical elements are not mentioned, only the impact of the writer's intent, which is, ultimately the acid test of good writing—the author's intent and the impact on the reader.

EXAMPLE 8.8: A Walk Through a Whole-Class Discussion Comparing an Excellent and Good Example of Writing

EXAMPLE 1	EXAMPLE 2
Daniel woke with *a start*. He hadn't meant to fall asleep. The fire had almost gone out and didn't give much light anymore. He crouched down and peered into the dark forest. *He couldn't see anything or hear anything*. Had it come back? Was it out there now, watching him with hot, murderous eyes?	Daniel woke with *a jolt* from a sleep he never meant to have. The fire had burned low. He crouched in the fragile shell of light and peered into the looming blackness of the forest. *He couldn't see anything, couldn't hear anything*. Had it come back? Was it out there now, watching him?

FIRST EXAMPLE	SECOND EXAMPLE	THINGS WE MIGHT POINT OUT BEYOND TECHNICAL FEATURES
Daniel woke with a start. He hadn't meant to fall asleep.	Daniel woke with a jolt from a sleep he never meant to have.	Why is *jolt* better than *start*? What image does it give you? What is the difference in meaning between "hadn't meant to fall asleep" and "sleep he never meant to have"? What does the word *never* seem to imply? How does the second sentence make you feel about his situation? What makes us feel uneasy in the words he has chosen?
The fire had almost gone out and didn't give much light anymore. He crouched down and peered into the dark forest.	The fire had burned low. He crouched in the fragile shell of light and peered into the looming blackness of the forest.	What information is unnecessary? Why is "looming blackness" better than "dark"? Is it more effective to tell us it's dark or show us? How does each word affect you? Which words give us a sense of his anxiety? How does the word *looming* sound? Would the words *approaching* or *gleaming* have the same effect? Why not?

(Continued)

(Continued)

FIRST EXAMPLE	SECOND EXAMPLE	THINGS WE MIGHT POINT OUT BEYOND TECHNICAL FEATURES
He couldn't see anything or hear anything. Had it come back? Was it out there now watching him with hot, murderous eyes?	He couldn't see anything, couldn't hear anything. Had it come back? Was it out there now, watching him?	What sense does the repeat and rhythm of "couldn't see anything, couldn't hear anything" give us? How would you say those words? What emotion do they convey compared to "he couldn't see anything or hear anything"? Which of the two last lines has most impact? Which makes you feel more uneasy? Should the writer always describe the terrible thing, or should it be implied and left to the reader's imagination?

After this discussion, presenting the class with further examples of excellence will yield a more powerful discussion because of what they have learned during this analysis.

Teachers have found that if you were to show, for instance, two or three short, excellent but all different examples (from last year's class), even if it is the same context as this lesson, analyzing them leads to students seeing that there is not just one way to write in this particular genre or nonfiction style. If they "borrow" some of the words or phrases they see, that is a mark of a good writer.

A key point in our understanding was when we saw the value of showing students *two pieces of writing in which the success criteria had been fulfilled but one is much better than the other* and asking, "If they've both followed the success criteria, why is this one better than that?" This helps students see that simply following the success criteria for writing is not enough—you have to focus on quality too. Claxton (1995) described this process as helping students develop "a nose for quality."

SUMMARY OF KEY POINTS

1. Process success criteria differ for fiction and nonfiction writing: fiction has optional success criteria whereas nonfiction has transferable skills with compulsory success criteria for the structure of the text only.

2. Editorial skills (grammar, punctuation, spelling, and handwriting) have compulsory rules process success criteria.

3. Students analyzing and knowing what excellence looks like cannot be underestimated for its value in raising the quality of children's achievement.

Mathematics 9

Planning Graphic

See the following graphic for planning mathematics learning intention
and success criteria (Example 9.1).

EXAMPLE 9.1: Planning Pathway for Any Mathematics Lesson

Is it skill (e.g., addition of two digits/calculating area of a triangle)? Is it knowledge (e.g., properties of shapes/pi/table facts)?

Decide success criteria

Key facts found in textbook or
knowledge organizer

Plan how to co-construct

(e.g., demonstrate at the document camera,
Did I do first? Next?)

Do they know it? Tests and asking, "What quizzes
reveal level of understanding?"

Success guaranteed if success criteria are met and key facts applied accurately

Posters

Every time we do mathematics . . .

Key facts . . .

Mathematics is a good example of starting point learning intentions that are broad and need careful breaking down, as teachers consider what students need to learn on the way and how that would look as learning intentions for individual lessons. Although higher achievers in mathematics sometimes feel that they don't need success criteria, it is important that they are part of their co-construction. Sometimes students have superficial knowledge, and the success criteria bring out the depth of their understanding.

Examples of Lesson-Based Skill Learning Intentions and Process Success Criteria

EXAMPLE 9.2: Mathematics Learning Intentions and Co-Constructed Success Criteria

---

We are learning to calculate the area of a triangle.

Process success criteria:

Remember to:

- Identify and measure the base and height.
- Multiply the base by the height, and divide by 2.
- Record in units squared.
- Check the answer by drawing a rectangle with the same height and width as the triangle, then halve its area—the two answers should be the same.

We are learning to share a quantity into a ratio.

Process success criteria:

Remember to:

- Add the parts (e.g., 2:3   2 + 3 = 5).
- Write each ratio as a factor (e.g., 2/5 : 3/5).
- Multiply each fraction by the whole (e.g., 2/5 of 20).

We are learning to put numbers to 20 in order.

Process success criteria:

Remember to:

- Start with the single number.
- Teen numbers all start with 1 in the tens column.
- Finish with the largest number.

Ashlie Griggs, District Mathematics Coach, Madison County Schools, Kentucky; Jennifer McDaniel, Math Specialist for the Kentucky Southeast/South Central Educational Cooperative

Ashlie Griggs, District Mathematics Coach, Madison County Schools, Kentucky

The following examples were created by Ashlie Griggs, district mathematics coach for Madison County Schools, Kentucky, and Jennifer McDaniel, math specialist for the Kentucky Southeast/South Central Educational Cooperative. This was their response to my request to include these process success criteria, after I gave them some examples:

> You prompted us to take a deeper dive and think about steps and strategies for students to achieve the intended learning. We also feel we were able to do this without compromising the productive struggle that students need to engage in their initial experiences. This prompted us to consider possible scaffolds that some students might explicitly need in reaching proficiency.

EXAMPLE 9.3: Examples of Teachers' Plans to Incorporate Learning Intentions and Success Criteria

	GRAPHING COORDINATES	**SIXTH-GRADE MATH— NUMBER SYSTEMS**
KAS(s)	Standard: (6.NS.6) Understand a rational number as a point on a number line. Extend number line diagrams and coordinate axes, using appropriate range and intervals, to represent points on the line and in the plane, that include negative numbers and coordinates. a. Find and position integers and other rational numbers on a horizontal or vertical number line diagram; find and position pairs of integers and other rational numbers on a coordinate plane. b. understand signs of numbers in ordered pairs as indicating locations in quadrants of the coordinate plane; recognize the similarity between whole numbers, their negative opposites, and their positions on a number line; ordered pairs differ only by signs and their locations on one or both axes.	
SMP(s)	• Use appropriate tools strategically (SMP.5). • Attend to precision (SMP.6).	

What	• I am learning to plot ordered pairs in all four quadrants on the coordinate plane.	
Why	• To be able to use maps and graphs to find a specific location, such as where the games are located in a store.	
How	**Remember to:** • Use appropriate tools to help locate a specific location that represents an ordered pair (SMP.5). • Be precise when writing an ordered pair for a specific point (SMP.6). • Appropriately label the quadrants on the coordinate plane. • Use the relationship between distance from zero for positive and negative numbers.	

(Continued)

(Continued)

Possible Scaffolds	• Prelabeled sheets with quadrant labels • Explicitly given tools instead of wide choice • Anchor chart/visual model for positioning of negative and positive numbers on both horizontal and vertical number lines

	SYSTEMS OF EQUATIONS BY GRAPHING	EIGHTH-GRADE MATH— EXPRESSIONS AND EQUATIONS
KAS(s)	Standard: (8.EE.8a) Understand that solutions to a system of two linear equations in two variables correspond to points of intersection of their graphs, because points of intersection satisfy both equations simultaneously; understand that a system of two linear equations may have one solution, no solution, or infinitely many solutions.	
SMP(s)	• Make sense of problems and persevere in problem solving (SMP.1) • Construct viable arguments and critique the reasoning of others (SMP.3) • Model with mathematics (SMP.4)	

What	• I can find and explain the meaning of the point of intersection for a system of equations. • I can find the solution(s) to a system of equations graphically.
Why	• So I can determine better deals when purchasing something, businesses use them to determine at what point they will be making money • They will be used in Algebra 1 next year to begin solving systems of inequalities.
How	Solve a system of equations by modeling the situation using a graphical representation (SMP.1 & SMP.4). **Remember to:** • Use estimation to find a reasonable solution. • Use tools from your tool box to refine their answer. • Label the parts of the graph accurately. Explain the meaning of the solution of the system to a math partner (SMP.1 & SMP.3). **Remember to:** • Use your strategy cards to choose a second strategy to prove your thinking. • Use your conversation cards to have discussions with your shoulder partners about different possible strategies. • Interpret the solution using the context of the problem.

Intervention When Students Need More Support

Although the success criteria in mathematics give all the key steps involved, they might need to be supplemented on the spot for some students.

Imagine the success criteria for *adding two-digit numbers on a number line*. We might have the following:

- Start from the biggest number.
- Jump in tens first (e.g., 36, 46, 56).
- Jump the ones next (e.g., 53, 54, 55).
- Record where you land.

Some students, however, might be individually asked, if the teacher sees some difficulty, to make extra recordings to keep track of their jumps or to use arrow marks on their jumps. It is better to have fewer main steps for mathematics success criteria, and then supplement them according to need, than to have an endless list of steps or ingredients that students can lose track of, find hard to read, or be intimidated by.

Worked Examples and the Use of Success Criteria

Cognitive science has been influential in how we teach mathematics to ease the cognitive load on our limited working memories. One of the key strategies is to use *worked examples* as a way of breaking mathematics into smaller, more manageable steps during the process of explaining and learning.

1. The first step is to silently write up a new skill that is the subject of the learning intention. We traditionally talk as we are writing or talk as students are trying to read a PowerPoint slide. This splits their focus, making it difficult to think about what is happening in the mathematics. So I might silently write up, for instance, the column method for subtraction of three digits with one decomposition needed, or a simple equation using x with a given value. The students are asked to watch as I slowly write this up, pausing at each step but not talking. It is not helpful to ask questions after each tiny step, as this distracts from the flow of the process in hand.

2. After I have finished the example, I then explain what I did or ask students to explain what they saw. I might ask why I did a particular thing to deepen their understanding.

3. So far this is known as "My Turn." I then write up an almost identical example, needing the same process, and this is "Your Turn." They now work on this example independently.

4. Students need three exposures to new learning to remember it, so this would be repeated several times.

5. An extension of the worked example is to ask students to write the steps beside the examples. This is particularly helpful for older children and can be used to check the depth of their understanding but also to use for mid-lesson learning stops. We take one student's worked example at random, place it under the visualizer or document camera, and read through together. The class is then asked to discuss if the success criteria are accurate, what is good, and what improvements could be made. This analysis resonates with all students in the room, either confirming their understanding or challenging and correcting it. The following is an example of a student's worked example from Langford School in London, with written explanations (see Figure 9.1). These are, of course, the student's own success criteria (called "What makes good" in this school):

FIGURE 9.1   Student-Generated Success Criteria

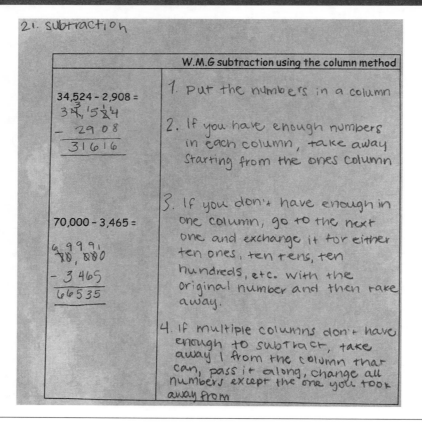

Don't Have Too Many Criteria!

One of the issues peculiar to mathematics seems to be the notion that every single step should be included, even when that mathematical skill has been known to the students for years. So, when measuring length, for instance, the key elements would probably be as follows:

- Start from 0.

- Record the exact measurement.

- Use the correct unit.

Video 9.1: Watch Seamus with eleven-year-olds, asking students to write their own success criteria for the mode and range.

It would be unnecessary to include getting the ruler, laying out the thing to be measured, counting along the ruler, etc., if those steps can be assumed for most students. Also, use the "Every time we do mathematics" poster for success criteria, which are common to all mathematics, such as "use your ruler to draw lines." If these are included in the success criteria every time, they distract from the key points or steps.

There are some mathematics lessons when success criteria are not needed, because they consist of knowledge input. I might, for instance, tell students that the interior angles of any triangle add up to 180 degrees then ask them to see if they can prove this. Success criteria are only useful if they give the key steps or ingredients needed to work through a skill or key pointers for knowledge. In this instance, there is only one piece of knowledge given, which is all they need for this task.

Incorporating Decision-Making

To incorporate decision-making, once students have mastered a specific mathematics skill, make the success criteria more open to students using their mathematical skill, as in the following example of subtracting two-digit numbers from each other on a number line:

- Decide which numbers and where to put them on your number line.

- Count between the numbers as efficiently as you can.

- Is your answer what you are expecting?

- Check your answers with your partner every so often, and make sure you agree on the answers.

Students Create Their Own Success Criteria

Feedback for closed skills focuses around mastery and checking for errors, reinstruction or more input, either from a peer or a teacher. Improvement is simply "getting it right," as there is no continuum of achievement with closed skills—only right or wrong elements. An effective technique once students can write independently and they appear to have mastered a particular skill is to get them to write out, in their own words, the success criteria for the skill so that they end up with the different criteria in one place in their books for future reference. This is particularly helpful and appropriate for secondary, middle, and high school students. This is also a good way to check for misconceptions. The best way I've seen this implemented is to do the following:

1. Ask the class to write the success criteria for the skill they've been learning about.

2. Choose one student's work at random to show their criteria under the document camera or visualizer.

3. The teacher reads them out and then asks, "Which of these have been done well, and is there anything that needs changing?" This is followed by talk partners' one-minute discussion.

4. Students give their feedback first about the successes and then what could improve the wording. A typical improvement suggestion is that there could be an example at the end of the success criteria to make it even clearer.

This routine is common practice in schools that used formative assessment as a minute by minute 'find out and improve' idea, not just for mathematics, but any piece of work where success and improvement feedback can be given.

From Specific Skill Teaching to Application Problem-Solving

Once students have *a range of techniques* for calculating a specific area of mathematics (e.g., addition), the learning intention and the success criteria become more choice oriented:

To add two-digit numbers

Choose from:

- A mental method
- Using a number line
- The column method
- Adding tens first, then units, then both together

What was once a specific learning intention (using a number line), once learned, becomes one of the success criteria for a more open learning intention. Success criteria often nest in this way.

If the mathematics was focused on a problem or word sum, even more open ended, again, although the answer must be right, the focus is now more likely to be the problem-solving strategies used, which will be reflected in the success criteria. Success criteria for solving a big problem, such as "How many minutes have you been alive?," might look like this:

To solve a mathematical problem

Choose from:

- Read the question carefully.

- Estimate the answer.

- What knowledge do you have that could help you (days in a year, hours in a day, etc.)?

- Talk through your thinking with your learning partner.

- Underline the key words.

- Choose a method—if multisteps, lay out each step clearly.

- Choose resources.

- Change your strategy if it doesn't work.

- Check your answer a different way.

- Compare your answer with your estimate.

 Video 9.2: Watch Susan asking sixteen- and seventeen-year-old high school students to use their success criteria to support their work on conics.

EXAMPLE 9.4: From Specific Skills to Open Applications in Mathematics

COMPULSORY SUCCESS CRITERIA FOR A SPECIFIC SKILL	OPTIONAL SUCCESS CRITERIA WHEN STUDENTS HAVE LEARNED A RANGE OF TECHNIQUES	OPTIONAL (BUT ENCOURAGED) SUCCESS CRITERIA THAT FOCUS ON PROBLEM-SOLVING PROCESSES AND DECISION-MAKING
To add two-digit numbers on a number line	To add two-digit numbers	To solve a word problem: How many hours have you been alive?
Remember to: • Start from the biggest number. • Jump in tens first (36, 46, 56, etc.) • Jump the ones next (53, 54, 55 etc.). • Record where you land.	Choose from: • A mental method • Using a number line • The column method • Adding tens first, then units, then both together	Choose from: • Read the question carefully. • Estimate the answer. • What knowledge do you have that could help you (days in a year, hours in a day, etc.)? • Talk through your thinking with your learning partner.

(Continued)

(Continued)

COMPULSORY SUCCESS CRITERIA FOR A SPECIFIC SKILL	OPTIONAL SUCCESS CRITERIA WHEN STUDENTS HAVE LEARNED A RANGE OF TECHNIQUES	OPTIONAL (BUT ENCOURAGED) SUCCESS CRITERIA THAT FOCUS ON PROBLEM-SOLVING PROCESSES AND DECISION-MAKING
		• Underline the key words. • Choose a method—if multisteps, lay out each step clearly. • Draw diagrams if it helps you. • Choose resources. • Change your strategy if it doesn't work. • Check your answer a different way. • Compare your answer with your estimate.

SUMMARY OF KEY POINTS

1. Class success criteria can be supplemented on the spot if an individual student needs more steps.

2. Use worked examples (My Turn, Your Turn), demonstrating in silence, to ease the cognitive load and make clear the steps.

3. Mathematics success criteria can be too lengthy; don't include every tiny step if that has been known for many years.

4. Decision-making can be incorporated into success criteria.

5. Once a skill is learned, older students can write their own success criteria for future reference and to check understanding.

6. Mathematics learning intentions move from specific skills to calculation using any method to problem-solving. The success criteria reflect the open or closed nature of the learning intention.

Science 10

The Planning Graphic

EXAMPLE 10.1: Planning Pathway for Any Science Lesson

Is there a transferable skill (e.g., write up an experiment; recording data for an experiment)?

Do you need to spend time on this, or have they used this skill many times and already know the success criteria? If so, ignore below . . .

Decide rules success criteria

Decide how to co-construct

Needs discussion about what a good one looks like (WAGOLL) using a model example

Success depends on:

a. Accurate use of any mathematical recording

What is the knowledge link (e.g., periodic table; parts of a plant; habitats)?

Decide key focus points (usually reference to key facts or where to find them) and show *next to* the skill success criteria for the lesson

b. If prose and knowledge are articulated correctly (writing quality)

From Primary to Secondary

Elementary/primary teachers tend to cover topics such as electricity, plant growth, life cycles, nutrition, exercise, materials, forces, and so on, laying the foundations for more complex science in secondary school. Sharing learning intentions in these early stages usually provides no problems, as they are not "giving the game away."

Here are some elementary learning intentions, which are designed to give students a repertoire of basic science knowledge to prepare them for deeper understanding in later years:

- We are learning to . . . know and label the parts of a plant.

- We are learning to . . . know how a circuit works.

- We are learning to . . . know the impact of exercise on the heart.

- We are learning to . . . know the different food groups.

The learning intentions are knowledge based, which is the focus of the teaching, but this knowledge, as in most subjects, is then applied via a transferable skill, such as being able to write an explanation or a description, label a diagram, create a poster, complete a graph of results, etc. These skills need to have equal status when they are being learned, and knowing "what a good one looks like" is a critical technique for improving student attainment almost immediately. By the time students are in secondary school, many of these skills have been well learned, but they still need to see how this content might look in a good example and—even better—if compared to a mediocre example. Always use anonymous work—preferably kept from last year—for these powerful whole-class discussions.

Giving the Game Away

Secondary teachers often worry that learning intentions in science give away the very result they want the students to discover during the lesson, such as the result of a chemical reaction. The key here is to rephrase the learning intention so that the discovery is still intact—e.g., "We are learning about the changes when water freezes," "We are learning how hydrogen peroxide reacts with potassium iodide," or "We are learning how aeroplanes fly."

In other words, the learning intention is faithful to the plan for the lesson and implies that there will be investigation and experimentation of some kind. It is then in the roundup of the lesson or lessons that the conclusions reached, and therefore knowledge gained, are made explicit—usually by the students themselves.

Examples of Science Learning Intentions and Success Criteria

The following are examples of science learning intentions and success criteria across the age range.

EXAMPLES 10.2: Science Learning Intentions With Related Content Knowledge and Success Criteria

LEARNING INTENTION	ACTIVITY	SUCCESS CRITERIA: PRODUCT AND PROCESS
To know the meaning of the terms *translucent, transparent,* and *opaque*	Shining light through materials	To show that you know the difference between the terms *translucent, transparent,* and *opaque* **Remember to:** <ul><li>Jot down the difference between the three terms (see the knowledge organizer).</li><li>Use the light source.</li><li>Look carefully at how the light shines on or through the material.</li><li>Decide which group the material belongs to.</li></ul>
To know the effects of exercise on heart rates To plan and conduct a fair test/controlling the variables in a science experiment (transferable skill)	Different forms of exercise agreed by the class	To show you know the effects and can plan and conduct a fair test **Remember to:** <ul><li>Create a recording chart for the different types.</li><li>Make a prediction.</li><li>Plan the fair test, making sure the variables stay the same except for one change each time (see the "Fair test rules" poster)</li><li>Keep a record of your results.</li><li>Look for trends, and make a hypothesis if possible.</li><li>Make a generalization if your hypothesis is correct.</li><li>Give reasons for your conclusions, and link with your prediction.</li></ul>

(Continued)

(Continued)

LEARNING INTENTION	ACTIVITY	SUCCESS CRITERIA: PRODUCT AND PROCESS
To know that some materials change when heated or cooled To draw conclusions reflecting results (transferable skill)	Find out what changes occur: making a cake, melting butter and cooling, frying an egg, heating and cooling water	To show you know the changes that occur with heating and cooling **Remember to:** • Keep a record of your results. • Read your results to check for sense. • Talk about what they show. • Decide what has changed or not and why. • Write a summary conclusion (see good example).
To know how to use arrows to represent forces in a diagram	Pictures of still and moving objects	To show you know how to use arrows to represent forces in a diagram **Remember to:** • Forces act in different directions (see the knowledge organizer). • The arrow shows the direction of the force. • Study the pictures carefully for the direction of the force. • Put the arrows in the correct place.
To be able to describe states of matter using particle models	Solid, liquid, gas card pairs	To show that you can describe states of matter using particle models **Remember to:** • Do an independent card sort. • Pair, then discuss different ways of organizing. • Re-sort if necessary. • Draw a particle model for solid, liquid, and gas (see example).

From the United States, Stephanie Harmon from Rockcastle High School in Kentucky produced the following science learning intentions and success criteria. The statement of the final outcome expected is broken down into "Remember to . . ." bullets although it is possible there could be further a breakdown depending on the needs of the class.

EXAMPLE 10.3: A Teacher's Plan for a Science Topic for Fifteen- and Sixteen-Year-Olds

Forces and Interactions—Universal Gravitation Learning Intention (Tenth Grade: Fifteen- and Sixteen-Year-Olds)

This unit deals with gravitation. Both learning intentions are centered around this. This lays the groundwork for understanding other inverse square relationships—particularly electrostatic forces (Coulomb's law).

	USING MATHEMATICS AND COMPUTATIONAL THINKING	HS FORCES AND INTERACTIONS
NGSS HS-PS2-4	**Use mathematical representations of Newton's Law of Gravitation <u>and Coulomb's Law</u> to describe and predict the gravitational <u>and electrostatic</u> forces between objects.** [Clarification Statement: Emphasis is on both quantitative and conceptual descriptions of gravitational <u>and electric</u> fields.] [*Assessment Boundary: Assessment is limited to systems with two objects.*]	
Science and Engineering Practices	Mathematical and computational thinking at the 9–12 level guilds on K–8 and progresses to using algebraic thinking and analysis, a range of linear and nonlinear functions, including trigonometric functions, exponentials and logarithms, and computational tools for statistical analysis to analyze, represent, and model data. Simple computational simulations are created and used based on mathematical models of basic assumptions. • Use mathematical representations of phenomena to describe explanations.	
What	I am learning to describe the gravitational force (F_G) between objects. I am learning to predict the F_G between objects.	
Why	So that I can explain the effects of F_G between distant objects Electrical forces are also represented by an inverse square law. Understanding the relationships between variables in determining the F_G will help build an understanding of the relationships between variables in determining electrical force.	
How	Describe how F_G changes as other variables (mass, distance) change. **Remember to:** • Use drawings as models to support your thinking. • Label the drawings to include how mass and distance are represented. • Use conversation cards to discuss changes in variables with your talk partner.	

(Continued)

(Continued)

	USING MATHEMATICS AND COMPUTATIONAL THINKING	HS FORCES AND INTERACTIONS
	Predict how the F_G changes. **Remember to make a prediction:** • When the mass of one object changes • When the masses of both objects change • When the distance between two objects changes • When both the distance between and the mass of one or both objects changes • For concepts of proportion • With supporting conceptual examples	
Possible scaffolds	• Anchor chart or visual model for inverse square patterns	

SUMMARY OF KEY POINTS

1. Basic science knowledge is the focus of primary teaching.

2. Learning intentions in secondary schools don't need to "give the game away" if worded as "We are finding out the impact/what happens when . . ."

History and Geography 11

Much of history and geography is applied by students in writing forms. The knowledge is usually part of the learning intention: it is what you want them to learn. Notice in the following examples the learning intention is appropriately knowledge based and the success criteria help students see what they need to do to achieve that learning intention in their written application. Missing from this example is some key focus points for the specific knowledge, but access to this varies in every classroom—students might have a textbook, some handouts, a displayed poster or the outcomes of a brainstorm, and so on.

History Examples

EXAMPLE 11.1: History Learning Intentions With Process Success Criteria Linked to Written Application

LEARNING INTENTION	CONTEXT	PROCESS SUCCESS CRITERIA
To weigh the advantages and disadvantages of different types of Roman government	Summarizing text and creating a timeline of government changes and key events + discussion and analysis, then presenting own conclusion in pairs	Remember to: • Describe each type of government. • Consider some of the pros and cons of each. • Consider which you think is best and why. • Share conclusions, and plan presentation.

(Continued)

(Continued)

LEARNING INTENTION	CONTEXT	PROCESS SUCCESS CRITERIA
To know the main elements of the feudal system	Given diagram of levels on worksheet + paired discussion	**Remember to:** • Complete the diagram showing the appropriate levels. • Discuss the interaction between the levels. • Use correct vocabulary. • Summarize the info for the feedback.

Geography Examples

EXAMPLE 11.2: Geography Learning Intentions With Process Success Criteria Linked to Written Application

LEARNING INTENTION	CONTEXT	PROCESS SUCCESS CRITERIA
To know ways of controlling drought	Savanna grassland	**Remember to:** • List the different causes of drought. • Explain how these could be reduced. • List your recommendations for how people can cope and live with drought. • Make comparisons with drought in the UK.
To understand the positive and negative effects of human activity on the environment	Tourism (research effects on St. Lucia)	**Remember to:** • Classify the positive and negative effects. • Discuss the negative effects, and think of a solution.

SUMMARY OF KEY POINTS

1. History and geography learning intentions are often knowledge facts applied via a literacy skill.

2. Key focus points or access to the related knowledge help anchor students' applications.

Examples From Other Subjects 12

This chapter includes examples from other subject areas that teachers have experimented with in my learning teams.

Art

Teachers sometimes think that creative subjects are impossible to create success criteria for, but it depends on whether students are learning a particular art technique, have knowledge about a particular artist, or whether the learning intention is creative. The following shows the difference:

The Planning Graphic

EXAMPLE 12.1: Planning Pathway for Any Art Lesson (Use the Same Ideas for Music Pathway)

Is it a skill? An art technique? (e.g., using watercolors; creating a wash effect; creating a collage; using perspective; using clay modeling techniques)	Is it knowledge? (e.g., the style and works of Van Gogh; cubism, pointillism, artists' inspirations)
Decide the steps or ingredients success criteria.	Teaching
	It is often combined with techniques training, so that students try to paint in the style of a particular artist, for instance.

(Continued)

(Continued)

Decide how to co-construct (e.g., demonstrating how to do it, asking, "What did I just do?" for each step)	
It is useful to show students a good example or photo from last year and one that's not good, or create these yourself.	
When combining a skill with creativity, the success criteria for the skill are applied but the creativity is in the student's own hands. Models of past students' work with some class analysis of what makes them good or not develops the idea of what good art might look like.	
Success depends on skilled application of techniques, but the subject matter depends on subjective opinion.	

Music

LEARNING INTENTION	CONTEXT	PROCESS SUCCESS CRITERIA
To understand and explain the use of musical instruments and elements in programmatic music	A chosen story: groups compose programmatic music	**Remember to:** • Create a balanced three-section composition. • Use tone, pitch, and dynamics to reflect the events and mood of the story. • Use the instruments creatively.
To be able to perform a piece of music as a group	Stone Age raindance/percussive instruments	**Remember to:** • Work cooperatively. • Decide structure (verse/chorus/repeats, etc.). • Check rhythm and pulse/speed. • Rehearse, going over any mistakes.

Drama

LEARNING INTENTION	CONTEXT	PROCESS SUCCESS CRITERIA
To be able to accept, respond, and reply creatively to Teacher in Role.	Pollution	**Remember to:** • Use appropriately adapted language and movement. • Use these to signify status and place. • Don't show embarrassment. • Sustain belief in your role. • Develop the situation through your contributions. • Move the drama on.

Design Technology

LEARNING INTENTION	CONTEXT	PROCESS SUCCESS CRITERIA
To develop quality control procedures for a product	Making a candleholder (Flowchart already given and discussed)	**Remember to:** • Add three elements to the flowchart that show that you are developing additional quality control procedures. • Produce a working drawing to illustrate this.

SUMMARY OF KEY POINTS

1. Creative subjects consist of specific skills and techniques as well as choice in how to apply them.

2. Techniques and skills need compulsory success criteria whereas design choices need discussion and examples shared and discussed about the concept of excellence.

Implementation

Whole-School Development 13

A Culture for Change

Andy Hind (2019) created the following table to show "the perfect school" in terms of the culture for the staff. The more embedded these elements are, the more successful any new initiative will be, as they embody *collective teacher efficacy (d = 1.39)*—the highest effect size in Hattie's (2009) *Visible Learning* (www.visiblelearningmetax.com).

Motivation of all individuals regularly monitored	Work/life balance encouraged and monitored	A culture of openness and security	Clear and agreed direction for future developments	Individuals demonstrate awareness and responsibility for development
Change handled effectively and welcomed by all	Clear and effective communication	Every member feeling valued and respected	Trust and challenge flow throughout	Shared and agreed values regarding core purpose

Openness is critical—appearing to agree during staff meetings but complaining in the parking lot is typical of school staffs where there is a lack of trust and people feel that they might be negatively judged if they speak out about things they are not clear about or have disagreements about.

When the school has trust and openness, I have found that negativity expressed about any of the elements of formative assessment—especially if they seem to fly in the face of everything we've been doing for years—is best dealt with by asking teachers to experiment, to see what happens. Perhaps most important, of course, is to provide teachers with the research evidence before embarking on any experimentation.

Support of School Leaders

It can be frustrating if, as a teacher reading this book, you don't have the support of school leaders to try new, tried and tested, evidence-based strategies. The best way to approach using co-constructed process success criteria, if this is the case, is to say that you want to experiment with this approach and that you want to give feedback on its impact as things develop.

Who Starts?

It has more impact if a few keen teachers first experiment with process success criteria, reporting what they have done and its impact at a weekly staff meeting. Asking all teachers to start something new, on the other hand, results in some paying lip service, some ignoring the "new thing" and a general lack of enthusiasm. Teachers on my teams have given feedback to their whole staff once every two weeks, simply saying what they have done and what the impact has been. Other teachers on the staff are much more likely to be interested if they hear the positive impact for their students in their context compared to hearing about success in different schools or countries to their own. They are also likely to come up to you after the meeting and ask for more information. Teachers will go above and beyond to help their students learn—but only if they believe it will be worthwhile.

After a few months of those keen teachers trialing, and whole staff interest has piqued, it is an appropriate time to lead on to whole school practice.

Time Between Trialing

Rushing this is not to be recommended, and it is better to ask teachers to choose one lesson in which they are confident to plan for process success criteria and choose a strategy for co-constructing. Teachers in primary/elementary usually start with English whereas secondary, middle, or high school teachers can take anything from their subject, usually just with one year group or grade, that they feel confident about breaking down into process success criteria steps or ingredients. After one lesson, this can gradually increase until, as many teachers after a year of this say, it becomes a way of working that you can't go back on, because you see the increase in student achievement.

Make sure teachers are given enough time to trial things before bringing them back together to ask for feedback. The first two weeks are usually difficult, and teachers need to "go through the pain barrier" until they have had time to sort out issues. I have had teachers on my teams say, "If you had asked me about this after two weeks I'd have been negative, but now I think it's fantastic." A month is minimum, with reminders to keep people on track.

Resourcing

Most of the co-constructing strategies require one or two examples of excellence and often a poor piece to use for comparison. One of the most valuable resources a teacher can have is first a visualizer or document camera, and secondly, a bank of old pieces of student work—many of which can be found on various online sites. If every time a lesson resulted in a product (paper, book, picture, model, etc.) you kept or scanned two excellent examples and one mediocre example, you would have, for next year's class, a wonderful resource for helping them not only generate success criteria but also for helping their understanding of what excellence looks like. Many examples are made up by teachers themselves, pretending that they are typed versions of a student's from last year. Whatever works!

Staff Meetings

The following elements seem to be helpful when planning staff meetings:

1. Distribute any preliminary research evidence, article, or chapter from a relevant book, and if possible, ask year groups or departments/faculties to have a premeeting to discuss what they have read. This takes teachers to a deeper level of understanding than if they are presented with something for the first time at a staff meeting. Give time for initial thoughts and reflections before the meeting. Give staff access to the video clips on my website (www.shirleyclarke-education.org) so that they can see process success criteria in action across the age ranges or grades.

2. Consider mixing up the seating in the staff room. One of the most successful formative assessment strategies is random learning partners who change weekly or every few lessons in secondary. This gives students a range of both social and cognitive partners over

a year and stops cliques and students being cast into "helper" or "helpee" roles for long periods of time. Teachers tend to sit in the same seats in staff rooms, often next to their friends, often who hold the same views as them! Teachers might have socialized with every member of staff but not actually discussed learning with them. Try random seating (numbers drawn randomly for numbered seats!).

3. When embarking on a new initiative like process success criteria, give the staff "reflection books" that they can use to jot down any significant things that happen during their experimentation—particularly successful lessons, quotes from students, etc. These can be brought to feedback meetings.

4. If the meeting is a feedback meeting, get teachers in groups (maximum six) with one person as the "scribe." This is the format I follow on my Day 2 and Day 3 learning team sessions, and it works well in generating discussion and input from everyone:

   a. I recommend two columns on each tablet of paper for each group: What We Did and Impact.

   Explain that instead of doing a round-robin, ask for one person in each group to start saying what they did and its impact (e.g., "I tried showing a good piece against a poor piece and co-constructed the success criteria with the class. The impact was that they followed the criteria while they were working") with the scribe taking notes; then see if anyone else in the group did the same thing or had the same impact. The scribe can then use tally marks in the margin to show the weighting of any statements. If someone had a different impact for this strategy, it is noted by the scribe.

   b. Give about twenty minutes for the group discussions, making sure all senior leaders stay away from the groups so that the teachers can speak honestly, and then ask for the scribe to read what has been written to the group so that they can cooperate in making sure the notes are representative of what had been discussed (give five minutes for this). Also ask each group to choose one good anecdote for their twenty-minute discussions, which would be useful for the entire staff to hear.

   c. Ask each scribe to read aloud, from their notes, to the entire staff. They then hand over to the person in their group with the anecdote who tells their story to the whole room. Each group does this in turn, with each scribe taking the lead. Allow more time for this group feedback to the whole staff; I usually find ten minutes per group is about right.

Clearly the number of staff alters the feasibility of this approach—as the more groups you have, the longer the second stage feedback lasts. A variation, but not as good, is to just have the twenty-minute group discussions, then someone collates all the pages from the various scribes for a second meeting in which the findings are read/distributed, and some of the anecdotes are presented by those teachers at that second meeting.

Timescale: What Should We Do First, Next, and So On?

- To begin with, staff need to be clear about learning intentions, knowing whether they need to be broken down for individual lessons and knowing whether they are skills or skills with knowledge applied. After reading the relevant chapter, you might need to have some staff meetings to be sure this is clear.

- The next stage is for each teacher to decide a lesson for which they can easily use one of the co-construction strategies:
  - Look at the planning graphic for your subject, and decide whether it is a skill (e.g., a mathematical procedure) or a skill with knowledge applied (e.g., a comparison of two poems).
  - Prepare the sources for the co-construction, or, if demonstration at the visualizer or document camera, plan what you will do.
  - Begin by explaining to the students that you are going to be helping them with their learning by trying something new and that you will be asking them afterward whether it was useful or not. *Obviously the age of the students matters in how much can be revealed. Also, if you are using the strategy, with young children, of showing them all the wrong steps for, say, counting, in order to get them to tell you what you should have done, you might want to leave the lesson to speak for itself. How well they do their own counting after the co-construction will be the acid test of the session.*

Continue to trial this strategy with different learning intentions before going on to another strategy. Primary teachers should stick with the same subject, trying the different strategies, before embarking on other subjects.

For most learning intentions, the chance to have a whole-class discussion and analysis of what a good one looks like (WAGOLL), and why it is better than a poor example, is a critical piece of the formative assessment jigsaw. Although it might seem burdensome to have to source resources, the benefits are immediately visible in the quality of students' work for that lesson, and you then have the resource for future use.

Whole-School Success

I have gathered the elements that successful schools seem to have in common when working together on formative assessment strategies, including process success criteria:

- Establishing aims and sharing interpretations of those aims

- Celebrating existing success

- Investigating children's understanding, rather than observing teachers, as a way to help teachers make changes without devaluing their practice

- Creating long-term plans

- Prioritizing and focusing on one aspect only (the learning can usually be applied to other areas as a consequence)

- Sharing responsibility for children's progress and teachers' progress with teachers

- Asking good coaching questions (e.g., "What were you pleased to notice about the children's learning in this lesson?")

- Supporting teachers in the early stages differently than those who are further along

- Conducting reviews by asking all involved, especially students, possibly using an anonymous online survey vehicle

SUMMARY OF KEY POINTS

1. The culture between staff members needs to be built on trust, respect, and openness in order to get the most out of any new venture.

2. School leaders have to share a vision of the power of formative assessment and be committed to supporting its development in as many ways as possible to maximize its success.

3. It is better to start with a few keen teachers trialing and reporting their findings back to staff on a regular basis rather than instructing all teachers to start at the same time.

4. Teachers need enough time between trialing and reporting to be able to ease in, go through stumbling blocks, and get to a point where they can confidently talk about the impact of the strategies on student learning.

5. All teachers need a document camera or visualizer in order to adequately co-construct success criteria.

6. Staff meetings need to be organized to allow that every person has the chance to give feedback and share findings (see previous text).

7. Teachers need to know what to do first, what to do next, and so on when embarking on trialing.

8. Schools in which these strategies have been most successful share some common strategies and aims for staff development, listed previously.

Teachers' Anecdotes About Implementing These Strategies

14

This chapter shows the impact of the various strategies used by teachers in sharing learning intentions and co-constructing success criteria as well as discussing what excellence looks like.

Anecdotes From Teachers in Learning Teams From 2017 Through 2020 . . .

The following stories are drawn from the most recent few years of teachers in my learning teams. They are anecdotes about the learning intention and process success criteria strategies they trialed and the impact on the learning. The full write-ups of every learning team can be found on my website (www.shirleyclarke-education.org) under Feedback from Learning Teams. These anecdotes are arranged in order of student age.

> *Using "Remember to" and "Choose from" works well. Students can be heard using these words and referring to them. The learning intention was changed from "I can . . ." to "We are learning to . . ." This was clearer for students and improved their self-esteem as they weren't faced with "I can" when at first they can't! They are now able to verbalize the learning intention more easily.*
>
> Paul Joyce, Norwich (Five-year-olds)

Having a "working wall" (Perspex-covered display board) next to the IWB (interactive whiteboard) has allowed me to add key points or steps from the lesson as it progresses. We can refer back to it and use our wall to inform the success criteria for the lesson. The children are part of the process, so they are more aware of the expectations and where they can look for support as they are learning.

Dai Jones, Earlsfield (Six-year-olds)

The context was World Book Day—the learning intention was to plan a design and the context to create a character from a book using a potato and scraps of material.

I drew a bad design, and the teaching assistant (TA) drew a good design. Talk partners co-constructed the success criteria for a good design by me asking the class to think of one thing that made the TA's example better each time. I used craft stick names for random calling, so no hands were raised.

After the success criteria were generated for a good design plan (legible, accurate scale, labels, etc.,) I took a photo of the whiteboard and uploaded it to Seesaw (a class app for student-driven digital portfolios and simple parent communication) with an audio recording of the success criteria to remind the students who found reading difficult.

Students' designs were of a high standard. They were motivated to create a good design using the co-constructed success criteria.

The students enjoyed all aspects of the task and were engaged throughout.

Tracey Williams, Ysgol Sant Dunawd (Six- and seven-year-olds)

I have different success criteria in a bag. Children discuss which are the correct ones. Children are developing more independence and reasoning why they think it should be a success criterion.

Wales (Six- and seven-year-olds)

I modeled robotic reading, then fluent reading, then discussed the success criteria for good reading. Students were able to rate each other, and individual students could identify an area of need based on the criteria.

Wisconsin (Six- and seven-year-olds)

In the first lesson on bar charts, we looked at an example of a graph and identified the features. These became our success criteria (e.g., scale, title, labelling the axes). After marking the graphs, all children had included these features but with some inaccuracies (e.g., scales drawn inaccurately, different width bars).

In the second lesson, we looked at an example of a graph similar to the one children had drawn. We discussed how this met the success criteria but not accurately. After this recap about accuracy, ALL children produced an accurate graph.

Emma Hancock (Eight- and nine-year-olds)

I used verbal success criteria, telling them what to do then having them repeat it back. They then successfully follow the steps. I came up with a song for rounding numbers.

Success criteria song for rounding:

Find your place, underline it

Look to the right, circle it.

4 or less, give it a rest

5 or more, raise the score.

Everything to the right becomes a zero

Everything to the left stays the same.

Kentucky (Eight- and nine-year-olds)

Success criteria enable children to identify errors at an early stage. One teacher described a less confident child saying, "Wow! I didn't think I could do such a good piece of work, and I got it finished!"

Stockport (Eight- and nine-year-olds)

Overheard from a group of low achievers in a mathematics lesson: "My answer's different to yours." "That's because you've missed out Step 2." There had been significant progress for all children as a result of being able to isolate exactly where they need to seek help or improve something.

Tunbridge Wells (Eight- and nine-year-olds)

I usually use two pieces of writing—one that meets the success criteria only and is quite basic and the other that is more detailed and includes excellence. Students then use a poster (generated by the class) with what to check for.

We use this:

S   Success criteria (Have I met these?)

E   Excellence (Have I included this?)

M   Myself (I proofread to myself.)

P   Edit (My partner and I edit together.)

Harry Brown, Sheffield (Eight- and nine-year-olds)

I created a checklist for adding decimals, asking children what they would need to do to be successful. This brought awareness to the process of adding. I can refer back to the criteria, and the students are more reflective about the process.

Wisconsin (Nine- and ten-year-olds)

I wanted the students to see that you have to go beyond simply using language tools in your writing, so I showed them three examples of writing that had all fulfilled the success criteria but were of varying quality. The whole-class analysis, deciding what made the difference between the pieces, really helped the students see not only what excellence looks like but how the tools are just tools. Students are able to be more selective of what they choose from the optional success criteria of writing tools.

Anne Smith, Wandsworth (Ten- and eleven-year-olds)

I focused on first thinking about the impact you want your writing to have on the reader. We were learning to write letters of complaint. This was the conversation between me and two students:

T: How do you want your reader to feel after they have read your letter? What would you like them to do?

Child 1:   I would like the reader to feel unhappy in a guilty way. I would like the reader to give me a full refund and sign up for a monthly health and hygiene inspection.

T:	*How would you achieve that?*
Child 1:	*I might use imperative verbs like "I demand."*
Child 2:	*I want them to feel ashamed of themselves. I want them to sack the person. I want a refund.*

The vocabulary and intent became clear to them, and they were able to list these as their own success criteria. This process positively impacted the finished letters.

Simon Collis, Sheffield (Eleven-year-olds)

In an art lesson, students looked at various drawings of people and were asked, "What makes this a successful picture?" They generated the success criteria based on the learning intention of correct proportions. This had a positive impact on the quality of the artwork, and they later transferred these skills in another task. The students developed their own shorthand success criteria.

Katy Tindall, Hertfordshire (Ten-year-olds)

Learning intention: To be able to write a clear set of instructions

Context: By making a box guitar (linked to science topic on sound)

After initial introduction to the learning intention, the children were shown three examples of eleven-year-old children's instructional writing and were given two minutes with talk partners to compile ideas about the features of instructional writing. Ideas were shared, and the success criteria (or X factor! in this class) were generated:

Success criteria generated by children:
• *Title*
• *What you need*
• *How to make*
• *Numbers*
• *Bullet points*
• *Verbs*
• *Time connectives*
• *Diagrams*

(Continued)

(Continued)

> The children were then given a poor set of instructions for making a box guitar and tried to follow them, annotating and making improvements to them as they proceeded.
>
> After a discussion about following poor instructions and how they could be improved, the children set about writing their own instructions. They were then able to make their own box guitars by following their talk partner's instructions. This allowed them all to peer mark their partner's work according to the success criteria.
>
> The lesson was extremely successful, and the children produced the best set of instructions they had all year.
>
> Kent (Ten- and eleven-year-olds)

> I worked with a student who lacked motivation in reading. I created a list of criteria and then checked off his achievements. The student was motivated to read to achieve his goals. He used the targets to improve his reading.
>
> Wisconsin (Ten- and eleven-year-olds)

> In one school, attainment levels went up from 87 percent to 92 percent. In this school, children ask for help and extra work for success criteria that they feel they have not achieved. This is seen as a huge leap in confidence from the previous mindset of "I'm no good at this."
>
> Scotland (Ten- and eleven-year-olds)

> We watched a video of a previous class's poetry performance (three groups) and generated success criteria from this. I asked the students how they could make their performances even better. Students gave ideas that were added to the criteria for performing a poem. This had an impact on the current class's performance, as it was higher quality. Excellent feedback was given to me from a schools inspector.
>
> Emma Shingle, Wales (Eleven-year-olds)

A child on the *Special Needs* registry said, "Do they do success criteria in secondary schools, because I really know what I'm doing with them?" In one IEP (individualized education plan) box, he had previously written "Not annoying people around me" in answer to "What helps you learn?" This time he had written "Success criteria help me learn."

Wales (Eleven-year-olds)

Before I worked with Shirley in the learning team, my school said we had to produce learning intentions slips and success criteria in advance for each lesson. I started co-constructing the success criteria with the students in mathematics and English, using good and bad examples or asking the students to solve a problem. They then generate the success criteria based on this (What did you have to do?), which is then written up on the board and kept displayed all lesson. There has been very positive feedback from the students. I am now applying this across the curriculum. One student said, "I like writing the success criteria together because it makes me feel more involved, and I can give my ideas."

Ann Smith, Gloucester (Twelve-year-olds)

I started the class by explaining that there was a hidden letter in the room. Even some of my most reluctant learners grew smiles on their faces and began to eagerly look for the letter. When the letter was found, a student removed the document, read the directions, and placed it under the document camera. The piece was an article with no text features, so we discussed what went wrong. The same piece with all text features was then displayed. A discussion followed on how the piece was more eye-catching, easier to comprehend, and how text features helped the reader. Upon this we generated success criteria on how to use the text features to better comprehend and utilize the information. They did this with a talk partner, and a representative shared the ideas as we generated class success criteria.

Daniel Hill, Kentucky (Middle school)

> *I had co-constructed success criteria with students using various strategies. Modeling what a good one looks like helped students to self-evaluate and has improved their confidence and self-efficacy. This led to engagement and ownership and raised awareness of the different steps in their learning. They now don't ask for as much help as independence is developing.*
>
> Wales (Fourteen- and fifteen-year-olds)

> *I presented the idea of quality, showed examples, and had students generate the criteria for what would make the project successful. The resulting quality of work was higher than in previous years.*
>
> Wisconsin (High school)

> *I had a constructed response completed by students under the document camera. They discussed what was good and bad about the constructed responses. They can now raise and correct their own.*
>
> Kentucky (High school)

Final Words

Although in the late nineties learning intentions and success criteria seemed a simple matter of telling children what they were learning and what they needed to do to succeed, I have been privileged to have been able to work with thousands of teachers on my courses and in my learning teams—all of whom have trialed and experimented with ideas to get to grips with learning intentions and success criteria. It is because of their insights and instructive feedback that new light has been shed on what works and what works better. The concepts and strategies in this book have all been developed from real teachers in real settings and have been replicated across the globe to give students more access to what used to be the secret world of the teacher's knowledge.

Whenever I think that learning intentions and success criteria have gone as far as they can, they seem to move on incrementally as we continue to learn more about the process of learning and what really helps children. Making knowledge equal to skills is probably the latest addition to my thinking, led by research and teachers' own realities, where we are now seeing that the knowledge really does matter and is not just a linking stimulus for developing skills.

Who knows where the practice of sharing learning intentions and co-constructing success criteria will take us next? It is always challenging—but always exciting and rewarding. Hearing feedback from teachers about their children's leaps in achievement because of the inclusion of process success criteria has been uplifting. I am forever indebted to teachers for their enthusiasm and commitment to the continual understanding of the power of formative assessment.

References

Ames, C., & Ames, R. (1984). Systems of student and teacher motivation: Toward a qualitative definition. *Journal of Educational Psychology, 76,* 535–556.

Black, P. J., & Wiliam, D. (1998a). Assessment and classroom learning. *Assessment in Education: Principles, Policy and Practice, 5,* 7–73.

Black, P. J., & Wiliam, D. (1998b). *Inside the black box: Raising standards through classroom assessment.* London, England: King's College London.

Black, P. J., & Wiliam, D. (2009). Developing the theory of formative assessment. *Educational Assessment, Evaluation and Accountability, 21,* 5–31.

Butler, R. (1988). Enhancing and undermining intrinsic motivation: The effects of task-involving and ego-involving evaluation on interest and performance. *British Journal of Educational Psychology, 58,* 1–14.

Chiu, M. M., Chow, B. W.-Y., & Joh, S. W. (2017). Streaming, tracking and reading achievement: A multilevel analysis of students in 40 countries. *Journal of Educational Psychology, 109,* 915–934.

Clarke, S. (2001). *Unlocking formative assessment: Practical strategies for enhancing pupils' learning in the primary classroom.* London, England: Hodder & Stoughton.

Clarke, S. (2014). *Outstanding formative assessment.* London, England: Hachette.

Claxton, G. L. (1995). What kind of learning does self-assessment drive? Developing a "nose" for quality: Comments on Klenowski. *Assessment in Education: Principles, Policy and Practice, 2,* 339–343.

Crooks, T. (1988) The impact of classroom evaluation practices on students. *Review of Educational Research, 58,* 438–481.

Deevers, M. (2006). *Linking classroom assessment practices with student motivation in mathematics.* Paper presented at the annual meeting of the American Educational Research Association, San Francisco, CA.

Dweck, C. (1989). Motivation. In A. Lesgold & R. Glaser (Eds.), *Foundations for a psychology of education.* Hillsdale, NJ: Erlbaum.

Gardner, H. (1993). *Frames of mind: The theory of multiple intelligences.* New York, NY: Basic Books.

Hattie, J. A. C. (2002). Classroom composition and peer effects. *International Journal of Educational Research, 37,* 449–481.

Hattie, J., & Clarke, S. (2019). *Visible learning: Feedback.* Abingdon, England: Routledge.

Hattie, J. (2009). *Visible learning: A synthesis of over 800 meta-analyses relating to achievement.* Abingdon, England: Routledge. Retrieved from www.visible learningmetax.com

Hattie, J., & Timperley, H. (2007). The power of feedback. *Review of Educational Research, 77,* 81–112.

Hillocks, G., Jr. (1986). *Research on written composition, new directions for instruction.* Urbana, IL: National Conference on Research in English.

Hind, A. (2019). Graphic seen on twitter @ andy_elearning.

Nuthall, G. A. (2007). *The hidden lives of learners.* Wellington, New Zealand: NZCER Press.

Oakes, J. (1992). Can tracking research inform practice? Technical, normative, and political considerations. *Educational Researcher, 21,* 12–21.

Paixao, L. (2013, October 29). *Embedded formative assessment: Great book!* Retrieved from http://lianepaixao.wordpress.com/2013/10/29

Ramaprasad, A. (1983). On the definition of feedback. *Behavioral Science, 28,* 4–13.

Rolland, R. G. (2012). Synthesizing the evidence on classroom goal structure in middle and secondary schools: A meta-analysis and narrative review. *Review of Educational Research, 82,* 396–435.

Sadler, R. (1989) Formative assessment and the design of instructional systems, *Instructional Science, 18,* 119–144.

Wiliam, D. [dylanwiliam]. (2018). Times educational supplement article [Tweet].

Wiliam, D., & Leahy, S. (2015). *Embedding formative assessment: Practical techniques for K–12 classrooms.* West Palm Beach, FL: Learning Sciences International.

Willingham, D. T. (2009). *Why don't students like school: A cognitive scientist answers questions about how the mind works and what it means for your classroom.* San Francisco, CA: Jossey-Bass.

Index

Confident Teachers, Inspired Learners

CAROL PELLETIER RADFORD

This vivid and inspirational guide offers educators practical strategies to promote their well-being and balance. Readers will find wisdom for a fulfilling career in education through teachers' stories of resilience, tips for mindful living, and podcast interviews with inspiring teachers and leaders.

JULIE STERN, KRISTA FERRARO, KAYLA DUNCAN, TREVOR ALEO

This step-by-step guide walks educators through the process of identifying curricular goals, establishing assessment targets, and planning curriculum and instruction that facilitates the transfer of learning to new and challenging situations.

STEPAN MEKHITARIAN

Transition back to school by leveraging the best of distance learning and classroom instruction. Learn how to create a blended learning experience that fosters learning, collaboration, and engagement.

SHIRLEY CLARKE

Learning intentions and success criteria expert Shirley Clarke shows how to phrase learning intentions for students, create success criteria to match, and adapt and implement them across disciplines.

To order your copies, visit corwin.com

No matter where you are in your professional journey, Corwin aims to ease the many demands teachers face on a daily basis with accessible strategies that benefit ALL learners. Through research-based, high-quality content, we offer practical guidance on a wide range of topics, including curriculum planning, learning frameworks, classroom design and management, and much more. Our resources are developed by renowned educators and designed for easy implementation in order to provide tangible results for you and your students.

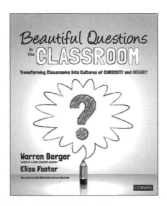

WARREN BERGER, ELISE FOSTER

Written to be both inspirational and practical, *Beautiful Questions in the Classroom* shows educators how they can transform their classrooms into cultures of curiosity.

ERIC M. ANDERMAN

Delve into the what, why, and how of motivation, its effects on learning, and your ability to spark that motivation using practical strategies to improve academic outcomes.

SERENA PARISER, EDWARD F. DEROCHE

Gain time in each day, reduce stress, and improve your classroom learning environment with 35 practical, teacher-proven strategies for managing time and setting personal boundaries.

CATLIN R. TUCKER

Balance With Blended Learning provides teachers with practical strategies to actively engage students in setting goals, monitoring development, reflecting on growth, using feedback, assessing work quality, and communicating their progress with parents.

A SAGE Publishing Company

CORWIN HAS ONE MISSION: to enhance education through intentional professional learning.

We build long-term relationships with our authors, educators, clients, and associations who partner with us to develop and continuously improve the best evidence-based practices that establish and support lifelong learning.